'I will read anything that John Summers writes. . . . Warm, enquiring, intelligent and authentic.' —Kiran Dass, *Kete*

'There is no other writer in New Zealand who can write so quietly; so much of *The Commercial Hotel* exists in the soft light of dawn, or twilight, due to the prose style and the tone it achieves.' —Steve Braunias, *Reading Room*

'A sparkling and enduring collection.' —Tilly Lloyd, Newstalk ZB

'Meticulously researched, gorgeously written and endlessly surprising, *The Commercial Hotel* is a compendium of sparkling oddities.' —Tom Doig, *The Spinoff*

'Nowhere is like anywhere else, and this collection shows us our own peculiarities from the inside, with a loving and observant eye.' —Tim Upperton, *NZ Listener*

'As a journey through odd by-ways of New Zealand life, this is a great collection from a writer who can see the importance of things we might otherwise cast aside.' —Nicholas Reid, *Reid's Reader*

'a pleasure to read' —Jim Sullivan, *Otago Daily Times*

# The Commercial Hotel

*John Summers*

TE HERENGA WAKA
UNIVERSITY PRESS

Te Herenga Waka University Press
PO Box 600 Wellington
New Zealand
teherengawakapress.co.nz

A catalogue record is available from the National Library
of New Zealand.

ISBN 9781776564217

Published with the support of a grant from

ARTS COUNCIL OF NEW ZEALAND TOI AOTEAROA


Printed by Blue Star, Wellington

*for Alisa and Henry*

# Contents

# On Coral Islands

Within minutes you could erect shelter. Rubbing sticks together was as effective as a cigarette lighter. Such tasks were difficult enough to be interesting but never onerous. And the temperature was always right for swimming.

*The Coral Island* was a Victorian novel full of Victorian values – I doubt it gets read much now – and it tells the story of three English boys stranded on a Pacific island. I say stranded, but this was survival as holiday. Some of the happiest hours of my childhood were those spent sitting on the mat, listening to a teacher read from this book. I went about for weeks afterwards craving breadfruit, imagining something between a baked potato and bread fresh out of the oven, and I dreamed of islands, failing to twig that I was already on a Pacific island. In my mind it was somewhere else. These South Seas were too close, too familiar. I wasn't entirely wrong in assuming it was elsewhere. The author, a Scot named Ballantyne, had never been to the Pacific himself. His account was make-believe, a cobbling together of everything he'd read. The Coral Island of the title was a veritable Pak'nSave, where the boys feasted on pigs, taro, yams, sweet potatoes, plums and sugar cane as well as 'cocoa nuts' that could be stuffed a couple at a time in pockets and then opened easily with a knife, the juice lemonade-like. It was a fantasy, and it was very much a white man's fantasy. These were not islands where people lived and worked to make a living, but background, a stage set with all the messy business of school and work and life excised. When the locals did appear in *The Coral Island* they were just as phoney as the cocoa nuts, the usual cannibals and noble savages of Victorian literature.

And yet, although I know all this now, islands still have their appeal. There is surely a direct line from Defoe to Ballantyne to the House of Travel, and despite my better judgement that line runs within my brain too. The sight of hibiscus stirs something between hope and yearning, emotions similar to those I felt sitting on the mat, listening to my teacher read. And I have holidayed in Sāmoa, Tonga and Niue, coming to see, in the limited way that a tourist can, the realities of island life – but also breadfruit in the wild, the opportunity to dispel that persistent myth, which is perhaps why I've never eaten it, have allowed it to remain the perfect fruit of my daydreams.

This is all to say that when, on another island holiday, this time in Rarotonga, I came across a battered paperback about a New Zealander who had lived alone for years on an uninhabited Pacific atoll, I had no choice but to read it, to let it creep into any idle hour's thought. I am far from alone in this. Tom Neale's *An Island to Oneself* was published in 1966 in England, and would be translated into French, German, Dutch and even Persian. It's out of print now, but there's a readership still. Reviews crop up on Amazon and Goodreads, and copies float, flotsam in secondhand bookshops. It's a short book considering the time it covers, but Neale doesn't muck around.

His prose is straightforward, as taut as he was – photographs reveal the physique of a coat hanger. He allows himself only a brief exploration of the impulse to spend so much time alone on Suwarrow (then known as Suvarov), an atoll in the Cooks, attributing much of it to the influence of Robert Dean Frisbie, an American author who once spent a year there with his five children. The rest is Neale's account of his voluntary marooning. Suwarrow's last residents had been coast watchers, two bored men told to look out for a Japanese invasion that never came, and Neale moved into the tin shack they'd left behind. He grew a garden, raised chickens and caught fish to feed himself and the two cats he'd brought. Easy to rattle off these tasks, but each was its own small feat. Establishing the garden meant hauling topsoil across the island and, once the plants grew, pollinating each by hand – there are no bees on remote atolls. It was ten months before Neale saw another person, and all up he was there, alone, for two years, only leaving on a trade ship after suffering from back pain, which in Rarotonga was diagnosed as arthritis. Reason to give it up you'd think, but he still craved his lonely island, and would have been back right away but for the Cook Islands authorities. They weren't keen on the idea of Neale dying by himself in a remote corner of their territory, and refused him permission to return on any of the local vessels.

And so he went back to his original occupation: keeping shop. He ran a general store, selling kerosene, canned beef and dry goods. Six frustrating years is what he'd call this time, describing 1950s Rarotonga as if it were an asphalt jungle. The cars at a nearby petrol station gave off stinking fumes. Life was governed by the clock, and he had to wear trousers – on Suwarrow he'd gone about in a hat and loincloth. Return would be a relief, and in 1960 he got around the authorities by travelling back to Suwarrow on a private yacht. He lived there for another two years, the time punctuated by the arrival of three castaways, a couple named Vessey and their young daughter Sileia, who were marooned when their yacht tore open against the island's coral reef. They lived with him for two months until all four were able to signal a passing New Zealand frigate. Neale left not long after their rescue, after more people arrived – pearl divers from the nearest inhabited island, Manihiki – and he learnt they would be returning regularly to dive in Suwarrow's lagoon. Other voices, turning his 'heaven into hell'.

Ballantyne's *The Coral Island* would be updated by William Golding as *Lord of the Flies* – bloodlust replacing all that breadfruit. And Tom Neale's book has been updated too. While in Rarotonga, I learnt that his daughter, Stella Neale, wrote an epilogue to her father's book that she hopes to publish one day. I got in touch, and she sent me a copy of her manuscript. It's a tender but clear-eyed document that tells another story – a family story that runs alongside the original tale of the man alone on the island. Neale had a son at the time of his first stay on Suwarrow, and by the time he left for the second he was married with two more children: Stella and her brother Arthur. The six frustrating years that he described spending stuck in Rarotonga were in fact six years with his young family. He was a very private man, Stella wrote. 'To explain a private matter was not who he was,' she offered as explanation for why none of this appears in her father's book, and her description of him is of a loving if reserved father who rationed sweets and taught her his own skills of self-reliance. He had her opening coconuts with a sharpened crowbar and cutting wood with an axe when she was still in the single digits. He was also a stubborn man, certain about how things should be done. A useful quality on a desert island, where self-doubt has time to grow into despair.

On Rarotonga though, within his marriage, stubbornness was its own treacherous reef. Neale insisted that his wife, Sarah, a Cook Islander twenty years his junior, travel to New Zealand to give birth to Stella and to visit a son she had there. But when she instead travelled to her own island, Palmerston, to visit her unwell mother, he withheld his money, effectively forbidding her from ever going to New Zealand and creating a distance between them. Together they had planned to go back to Suwarrow with their children, like the Swiss Family Robinson, except that a coral atoll had always been Sarah's home. She was a great cook, Stella wrote, masterful at preparing fish, and had the skills to cope with the demands of a place like Suwarrow. But by the time Neale had organised his return, the marriage had broken down. He went alone.

Islands were where Neale would always go. Born in 1902, he grew up in Wellington and Greymouth and in his teens joined the navy on that old promise of seeing the world. But the glimpses it gave him, of South Pacific port towns and harbours and bars, weren't enough to sate him, and he left to wander the Pacific himself. For over a decade he island-hopped, living simply, picking fruit from the trees and taking odd jobs clearing bush or cutting copra when he needed money. These years of his life we might picture via Somerset Maugham: Neale as a character in the Pacific he'd described, perhaps invented; the beachcomber in that world of traders and tramp steamers. He returned to New Zealand once during this time – 'Which Tom?' his father had said when he'd called – but was soon drawn back, first to Moorea, where he settled for a time, and then to the Cook Islands, where he took that storeman job, working on some of its scattered islands. These are still remote places, reached only by small planes and infrequent ferries. Imagine how small, how sleepy they were then, in the late 40s and early 50s. Even so, Neale craved something quieter, a place where there truly was no sound beyond the waves, the birds and whatever noise you made yourself.

Islands loom even in his reading. He was a devotee of Conrad, Defoe and Stevenson, as well as Frisbie. 'No desert island story is altogether bad,' wrote George Orwell, 'when it sticks to the actual concrete details of the struggle to keep alive.' It could have been Neale's mantra – his own book was almost a manual on desert island life for all the information it contained. It covered what to take (tools, bandages, canned food and flour, six pairs of tennis shoes for walking on the reef), and how to strengthen a shack against tropical storms. It's not very well written, two people told me. But both had read it; both were recommending I read it. I wonder whether they would have suggested it so readily had Neale allowed himself a florid writing style or lengthy observations on his lust to be alone. That's what I tend to think we'd have if this book had been written now. Another story of someone finding themselves, of using some exotic place as a way to hit reset on their life and rethink their values. Everything left behind – the children, the marriage – would be there to provide the right context to their journey of self-discovery. While Neale does give some background about his life before Suwarrow, obviously what he shared was only a sliver and even that is rushed. It's as if he feels no need to convince us, knowing we're reading because we're there for the island already. Our daydreams are his, and all we want is to hear from the one man who has acted on them.

That's not to say the book is without drama. The stakes were incredibly high, because for all those tennis shoes, one thing Neale never took was a radio. He planned to live or die by self-reliance alone. At times, the odds were on him dying. The back pain that ended his first stay was so severe he was forced to his bed, and lay there unable to move with only two coconuts for sustenance. Straightforward he may be, but Neale describes these dreamlike days of pain vividly, better for his plain-spoken style – you feel sure he's telling it as it happened, knowing he's not prone to exaggeration. He survived only through the most incredible luck. On the fourth day, while he lay there weak, a man walked in the door. An American, a Rockefeller in fact. James Jr, a scion of that wealth-dripping family, had been travelling the Pacific by yacht when he decided, out of pure curiosity, to pay a visit to what he thought was an uninhabited patch of sand. Rockefeller and his travelling companion stayed with Neale for a week, and nursed him back to health, rubbing his knotted back with liniment each evening. When it came time for them to leave, they organised for a trade ship to pick Neale up and take him back to Rarotonga.

So there is drama there, and yet it is all of the island. Neale wrote of feeling fatherly towards Sileia Vessey, the daughter of the two castaways, but never described what it must be like to leave your own two children on the docks without knowing when you'd see them again, nor how the desire to see no one but your wife and children might turn into a wish to see no one. Maybe we'd have a better book had he explained this; maybe we'd have a worse one, an attempt to defend the indefensible. As it is, what we have is a story self-contained. Like an Agatha Christie, a puzzle to be solved in the company of the reader. Even with Stella's epilogue, we'll never know if

Neale truly found his peace on Suwarrow, but while reading his book we can have it for a moment ourselves.

Neale's time on Suwarrow didn't end with his book. In 1967 he went back, his supplies paid for with the royalties, and stayed for another ten years. Stock phrases come to mind: the island drew him back, had him in its spell. This is how he himself characterised his wish to be there, as if he were in thrall to the beauty of white sands and pale blue seas. There is no reason not to take him at his word, but surely it was aloneness too that spoke to him over and over. It was the main feature of Suwarrow after all and, maybe, for a man so set in his ways, aloneness meant beauty too, perfection. Things could be exactly as he wanted them, without the need to compromise or the risk of discord. When Stella came to visit him in these years, she found him fastidious still. Firewood was stacked neatly, and a shower was rigged outside. He fussed to organise his mail, and painstakingly wiped down his frying pan after serving a meal of cooked eggs. By then, Stella had taken a path the reverse of his, leaving the islands for landlocked Hamilton, where she trained to be a nurse. When she paid him that visit, he was shocked, in disbelief she'd come that far for him – just as his own father had been when Neale returned from the islands all those years ago.

Over those ten years, Neale became a mascot for dreamers like himself. People sought him out, travelled over oceans to learn from his example, to see what their own dreams looked like in reality. Germans were particularly keen, it seemed, and at one point he was filmed for German TV. And it was in the company of another man who had gone to the Pacific to enact a fantasy that Neale would end his days. In March of 1977, the crew of a visiting yacht found Neale suffering stomach pains and a ship was diverted to take him back to Rarotonga. There his pain was diagnosed as cancer, and he was cared for by a specialist named Milan Brych. Infamous now, Brych was a Czech who had fled his own country for New Zealand after the Soviets invaded. He could cure people, he claimed, using apricot kernels. It was a lie upon a lie. His qualifications were fake. He'd been in prison in the years he'd said he was studying. After being forbidden to practise in New Zealand, he had travelled on to Rarotonga, where he set up shop again. People followed him there – New Zealanders and Australians, hoping for their problems to disappear beneath the coconut palms. They would come to rest in what is known now as the Brychyard, not far from Neale's grave in Rarotonga's RSA cemetery, their graves recently restored after some were lost, washed away by the lap of rising seas. The vulnerability of islands.

Stella was with her father for two weeks before he died. She had heard he was ill and travelled back to Rarotonga, only to find him anxious that she not miss any of her studies on his behalf. Suspicious of Brych, she urged her father to seek treatment in New Zealand, but that was the rat race he said, and he refused to leave the islands. It was a difficult time. Later she'd realise he didn't want her to see him unwell, but back then they formed a truce of sorts, him insisting again and again that she forget him and go back to her studies, and her agreeing to leave at the end of the two weeks she'd booked. It meant that she was back in New Zealand when she learnt he'd died, and even then the news came late – he was already in the ground. Her epilogue doesn't describe their last moment together, but it does include the story of another farewell, one from the visit she made to Suwarrow. She hugged him on arrival then, to his surprise. He was never an effusive man. When they posed for a photograph he stood rigidly, her arm around him. It was when she was back onboard the ship, the engines pushing her away, back to Rarotonga, that he came down onto the beach with a cloth tied to a stick and waved it wildly. He waved it for as long as she could see him, as if only with the ocean widening between them could he show his love. And she waved too, grabbing a shirt from her bag. For as long as they could see each other they waved.

# What You Get, What've We Got

I do most of my writing on the Wairarapa line, the WRL. Every morning, every evening, it rattles beneath the hills between Wellington and Greytown with me aboard, tapping away, reading sometimes, often having a sly snooze. For several months of the year the view is of the dark, the windowpanes so black that you don't know when the tunnels have stopped or started. I wrote a ghost story on mornings like that, something I would never have considered before, but which seemed like the only response to the blackness out the window.

Alisa and I moved here from Wellington years ago. For her there was a job at the local paper, and for me small towns have always held a fascination, something, like a lot of things, that can be traced to childhood, to the time I spent in a small town on the edge of wheat fields blow-dried by nor'westers. My father lived there and once a fortnight I'd stay for the weekend, spending years parcelled out two days at a time. I loved it and I hated it. Dad didn't own a TV and there was always work to do. In winter the ground froze, and his big old house was cold the second you moved away from the fire. But then there was a fire, and I spent hours in front of it, reading his books, feeling them more intently somehow, the quiet and the isolation creating blank space around each word. I liked the small discoveries I made in this town, the mossed-over gravestones behind the church, the paper road that snuck through someone's section, and the way people had conversations not looking at each other but at some other thing, a trailer or a pig maybe.

Greytown isn't like that. 'Pretty bougie,' someone said to me the other day, and I couldn't disagree. You can pop into Saluté for pan-fried fish with cauliflower purée, saffron mayo and micro greens. But beneath the cafés and home décor stores it has the same bones as every small town – the main drag with a church and a dairy, a pub that sells beer in big brown bottles. The bus driver will chat at length about painting his house or growing asparagus before detouring to drop me at my front gate, and in the working men's club a man named Brush told me a story about assembling cars, back when that was still done in this country. The gist of this was that he was sent to Japan to learn how it was that they made thirty Toyotas a day while we only managed three. He flew there, had a great time beneath the cherry blossoms, and visited a factory where, when the whistle blew for smoko, the men sprinted to their break area, sucked down a cigarette before sprinting back to the production line. The 'learnings' from this trip? Yeah, nah. The New Zealanders would stick to three. I repeat this because I suspect it isn't a story someone would tell in the city, at least not the way Brush told me. The moral, that we'd rather take our time, would become a caution there.

Alisa and I live here in a house that had belonged to a man taken by dementia. He was probably responsible for the river stone wishing wells in both the front and back yards. He was almost certainly responsible for the scribbled family tree I found in a wardrobe, with a branch given to Sherlock Holmes. It's on the east this house, so that on leaving each morning I turn a corner and there, as if at the end of Kuratawhiti Street, are the Tararua Ranges, in mist sometimes, white in winter. 'There is a saying here if you see / snow on the mountains, frost / is what you get, and what've we got.' Pat White wrote that. Poet, painter, biographer, and the friend of a friend – when we made our plans to move here, he was the only Wairarapa writer I knew of. Probably the only one, I guessed. It was the country after all. Culture would mean A&P and Golden Shears, or the crafty stuff they sell weekenders. By the time we got here though, Pat had gone, leaving me to discover his lines in the Masterton Library, and to learn how wrong I was. One of Alisa's early jobs was to interview Joy Cowley. That's national treasure Joy Cowley, whose work has been read by generations of children, and who wrote one of our best stories, a cut jewel, 'The Silk'. Turns out she lived just up the road in Featherston. It was Featherston too that launched itself as Booktown, annually inviting local writers as well as visitors to talk about books beneath the sepia photographs of bearded worthies in the town hall. And I would find writers elsewhere, everywhere. One Sunday, I joined a fair-sized, appreciative crowd who had left their homes on a sunny afternoon to sit and listen to two visiting poets in Carterton's town hall. At home, I would open a literary journal to read a poem by someone whose bio note explained him to be, like me, a resident of Greytown. I say opened, but I didn't need to go that far – the cover was by a guy from Featherston. Since then, I've learnt the region is home to journalists and romance novelists, and an author shortlisted for the Booker.

I've only really flitted about the edges of all this, still an outsider after all these years. Too busy moseying about, my chief occupation here. I like to drive between the towns spread like islands along State Highway 2, admiring the firewood stacks and junk shops, the terrifying Kiwi gothic façade of Carterton's Royal Oak Hotel (it's actually quite nice inside). In the Featherston RSA, beer is served in handles to men and in tall glasses to women. And I can never walk past the noticeboard at Fresh Choice without reading its ads for bricks, firewood and puppies, and once, 'How to grow a great beard And trim it to please the ladys'.

In the warmer months, the days go on and on and on, and finally, the light creeps back so gradually that for a moment, the trees, the lawn and the leaves look dark and potent against the day. It's then that I like to sit in the conservatory someone has amateurly tacked to the back of the house and look out at my yard. The people behind us have let their garden overgrow and their two dogs roam, making tracks in the tall grass, and at that strange hour it seems to be overflowing, a swamp, a forest, or some other kind of old, unknowable nature coming over the wire fence and through the cabbage trees to take over, claim it all back.

I've always thought it was the open spaces of this place that have trained my eyes to see these things, to pay attention. But it's probably just the newness. For so long I had been bored, always thinking about the next place, another place. I grew sick of Wellington. Things there that once seemed surprising became wallpaper. I had stopped noticing, and so, for all intents and purposes, I threw a dart at a map. We left to spend a year in a heaving city beside the Gan River: Nanchang, China. There I got what I wanted. At once it was shocking, different and new: an old lady walked down the street with a bag full of live frogs, a rat scurried across the floor of the local pool hall while a man hitched up his pyjama pants before taking a shot. But eventually, we were just waiting behind these people in the supermarket queue, paying the power bill, forgetting to buy laundry powder. I wrote most of my first book in Nanchang, a kind of memoir, and I wrote a handful of travel stories too. Although in a way it's all the same; everything I wrote was a travel story of sorts. I don't mean they're all five things to do in Paris, but that they're stories about a time and a place and encounters. Even that ghost story I mentioned earlier was about these things. This was writing fuelled by the noticing I like to do, and it's possibly the reason I haven't tried harder to find other writers out here. Travellers hate the sight of their fellow tourists after all.

We don't have a reason to stay in the Wairarapa anymore. Officially we're here because of Alisa's job at the paper, the need for her to commute to Masterton. But she's moved on from that, and has begun to get the train to Wellington every day with me. And so even as we repaint the house and strip old wallpaper, we talk about how this doesn't mean we'll be here forever. Staying put is dangerous. It ends in wishing wells and family trees. And yet, the days continue to come and go, and on the Sunday of a long weekend, when the cars are bumper to bumper down the main drag – it's Highway 2 as well – the drivers tapping the dash as they hurry back to Wellington, I watch from the footpath, standing, still here.

# The Dehydrated Giant

One summer we drove east, beyond Gisborne to the quiet bays on that coast: Tokomaru, Tolaga. Towns where sand settles between the stones in the asphalt and, walking down the street, you're as likely to be passed by a kid on a horse as by a car. There was a campground we planned to stay at, but it was a treeless field. No toilets, no kitchen. 'We're pretty relaxed around here,' the owner said, but we weren't, so drove on to another. After pitching the tent, we walked to the end of the bay and onto a dilapidated wharf to look out at the empty sea – no ship had docked there for decades. We inspected a brick and concrete building, caved in at one side and crumbling. Grass grew in and around it. Close by were more of the same. The sea air had rendered them all dull and chalky, turning them into part of the landscape, unremarkable to the locals. These buildings were the old freezing works, and all that remained there of an outpost of an empire, an enormous meat trade that once meant there were works like these in every corner of the country. Like any empire, it had its own creation myth. Its Romulus and Remus were two Scots entrepreneurs, Thomas Brydone and

William Soltau Davidson, whose ship, the *Dunedin*, would be the first to carry refrigerated New Zealand meat to England. The frozen lambs they'd stowed aboard would sell there for twice what they would have got back home and received favourable mention in the *Times* and the House of Lords. A trajectory of plenty was born. By 1900, we were exporting more than three million sheep a year. When the chairman of the Meat Board retired in 1980, he was given a necklace of chop bones as a goodbye gift.

The other thing we know of all empires is they fall. There are still some freezing works left, but it's not the industry it was, not the one that had us striking a deal where England bought all the meat we had to sell. Historian James Belich writes of a complacency that came with that ready demand. For a long time we made little effort to pursue other markets; our first trade envoy to Japan didn't speak the language, could barely order a cab. So when the English began looking to Europe for their meat, taking the first steps in the experiment they are now attempting to undo, we were left with no ready replacement. England joined the European Economic Community in 1973, and still the freezing works rattled on, propped up by subsidies. The plaster was ripped off in the next decade, when the Lange government removed those subsidies and allowed competition from imports. From 1980 to 1995, there was a roll-call of freezing works closures: Southdown, Picton, Petone, Pātea, Shortland, Whakatū, Islington, Burnside, Westfield, Waingawa, Tomoana, Aotearoa, Feilding, Whāngārei and Kaiti. When people talk about the freezing works now, they're mostly talking about things that are gone.

Who mourns that old business of slaughter? You'll find those Tokomaru Bay buildings on the website of Heritage New Zealand, listed as a category two historic place. When the Pātea freezing works closed in Taranaki – an event akin to natural disaster, warned a government report at the time – the local historical society pushed to have the chimney preserved. It would be a monument, said society president Jacq Dwyer, but their plans were foiled when the council blew it up early one morning. So instead, Dwyer and her society created a small museum to the freezing works. Two old refrigeration compressors, a mannequin dressed as a butcher, a collection of old photos and half a dozen fibreglass sheep in what used to be the town's ANZ bank. One closed business within another.

From this distance it can seem an odd thing to commemorate. Don't freezing works float on a puddle of blood, sit atop a hill of bones? Arguably, our most memorable music video is 'AFFCO' by punk group the Skeptics, which was filmed at Auckland's Westfield works. It shows sheep being stunned and slaughtered mechanically like lids being fastened to jars. Front man David D'Ath sang while smeared with blood (actually food colouring and baby oil) and bound in cling-wrap. It was enough to turn people to vegetarianism, although director Stuart Page said later they were simply trying to document a part of New Zealand life: the killing chain. TVNZ recognised this, noting the video's 'everyday scenes at freezing works', before refusing to broadcast it. On YouTube it still carries a content warning.

I asked Dwyer about the impulse to preserve and commemorate an industry too gruesome to be shown on TV. She spoke about the need to do something with those compressors, how valuable they were; then, when I asked again, how out-of-towners wanted to see something that represented the old freezing works. I was being unfair really, looking for her to articulate the things I wondered about, to do the job I should be doing myself. For a long time, I'd toyed with the idea of writing a brief history of the freezing works in this country. It seemed strange no one had done so already. There's a history of New Zealand kitchens, and of comparatively young industries like wine, but no definitive book on the freezing works, a place where so many New Zealanders spent their days. I collected what books there were, such as *Meat Acts*, a 1999 volume commissioned by the NZ Meat Producers Board to commemorate its 75th anniversary in 1997. The book that came closest to what I wanted to achieve, but which focused only on the East Coast, was Sheridan Gundry's *Making a Killing*. (These titles! See also Peter Norman's freezing works memoir *The Meat in the Sandwich*.) I made a list of some of the points I would include – the voyage of the *Dunedin*, but also the next ship that sailed from Port Chalmers with a bizarre cargo of dead things: sheep, beef and pork, of course, but also barracudas, pūkeko and a cask of penguin skins. And another list that seemed to encapsulate the aspirations and appetites of an era – the meal we dished up to the Shah of Iran in 1974 as part of those patchy efforts to woo new markets: roast baby lamb garni, crown roast lamb in aspic, lamb medallions madelon and roast leg of lamb, as well as beef, turkey and chicken. But despite my list-making, I never got much further, rewriting the same three paragraphs every few months. I'm not a historian and had no real interest in putting in the hours that would be needed among the archives and microfiche readers to write this book.

Within my mother's family, the freezing works were both long gone and never far away. We dried ourselves on blue towels embroidered with New Zealand Refrigerating Co; I still have, in my kitchen drawer, a mean, wood-handled butcher knife that holds a good edge. To spend any time at all with my uncle or grandfather was to hear the works mentioned, and just like that: 'the works'. It was assumed you knew they were referring to the Islington freezing works, just beyond Hornby where they lived. My grandfather started there following a joinery apprenticeship, which he spent building state houses. Three government-issue saws would always hang in his shed. Once he got to the works he stayed until the day my grandmother brought in a cake for his retirement. The works had paid for his home in Hornby, the trip he took to Sydney for his son's wedding and the superannuation scheme that would let him prune roses and potter in his garage during his last years.

Often, on the weekend or after school, I'd prop my bike against the tin walls of that garage and wander in, inhaling the scents of turned wood and blood-and-bone fertiliser. He was a genial if reserved man; a smile and a nod told you he was pleased to see you. I usually turned up with some idea about building something: a CD stand, a toolbox, maybe. What a pain I was, I now realise. But he never said so, just wandered out to his timber stack to see what might be suitable. Building the thing would be his job too, but for the most basic tasks. That state-house apprenticeship had given him a wizardry with tools. Look at a carpenter's plane as if you've never seen one before. Could you guess that in the right hands, my grandfather's thick hands, it could make a rough, wide old board perfectly flat on every edge? I hung about, in theory, to learn some of these skills. In truth, it was his presence I was seeking. In that shed crowded with oiled tools and old things, the anxieties of School Certificate maths, schoolyard hierarchies and my looming, uncertain future all shrank and went still. He and I worked, for the most part, in silence. Our soundtrack was the slick-slick of the plane. Now and again, I'd break it to ramble on about something I'd seen in a book on carpentry. He'd listen, seemingly interested, although it must have been like Stephen Hawking having someone tell him there are these things called black holes. While he wasn't a big talker, occasionally he told me some story of his own. 'There was a fella at the works,' is how these yarns all started; they usually contained a description of a job done well and, although he never extracted it, a lesson of some kind. In one story, I remember the 'fella' was his first foreman. My grandfather designed and made a wheelbarrow that would be better suited to the freezing works than the ones they were using, but the foreman told him it was useless, and cast it aside. Later, a man from another department found it and asked for four more. Because this story highlighted his own abilities, I wouldn't say it was typical of the genre, and it's telling that he tried to present it as about the foreman rather than himself. Maybe that's the reason I remember it. So much else of our time together has faded, and I find myself ten years after his death mourning again, this time for my memories as well as the man himself.

To write about the freezing works, I also needed to talk to my Uncle Dale. My conversation with him was a reminder of how they both spoke. 'The works had its own lingo,' Dale told me, explaining that the expression 'The gun's gone off' meant the killing chain had closed and the men who staffed it would need to look for another job until the next season. But I suspected that while you might trace this lingo to the works, you couldn't say it stayed there. It was of them and their world more generally. 'All hair-cream and no socks' was an expression I'd heard Dale use. 'He'd done a stretch in the chokey' was another, describing a man they worked with who was either a thief or at least knew how to get his hands on things. Within these stories, the man in question almost always had some nickname. A laundryman was 'Willy Shrinkem', and a small man who liked to pick fights became 'the Dehydrated Giant'. There was 'Hot Foot', 'Biggie Rat', 'Sleepy Fox', and also 'Death', which sounds like a bizarre thing to call someone, but probably makes a lot of sense in a slaughterhouse.

It would make sense, too, in a Ronald Hugh Morrieson novel. The freezing works lurk in his *Pallet on the Floor* as a source of gothic horror, a place that leaves a psychic stain. 'So you were in Belsen huh?' reads the graffiti on the freezing works walls. Read now, the works operate in his book as a symbol of all that was wrong with that old, macho New Zealand, the violence that ran beneath the puritan society. The bad old, good old days, where toughness and mateship left little room for difference or vulnerability.

And yet, both my uncle and my grandfather spoke of the works, if not fondly, with nostalgia. It helped perhaps that neither had been in the business of killing animals directly. My grandfather began in the carpenters' shop, making the wooden chutes and the boards on which men scraped out intestines for sausage skins, as well as those barrows, and even, on occasion, wooden salad bowls to be gifted to visiting executives. From there he moved to the bag room, where they made and printed the cloth bags used to wrap frozen meat. My uncle joined him there later. He had also done an apprenticeship, as a mechanic. But with a young family, he wanted something better-paying, and for a long time for a lot of men nothing paid better than the works. He started in the yard driving forklifts and doing odd jobs. He worked as a butcher's labourer in the beef house for a while, sawing brisket with a handsaw. 'Jesus, sweat!' he said of that job. 'Because of the heat of the beast.' Eventually he joined his father in the bag room. Dale repaired sewing machines and printing presses; he cut stencils and type for printing bags, learning to cut it backwards, a mirror image. It got so that signing a cheque he had to think which way to write.

Hearing about these jobs of theirs and the others they described left me with the impression of the works as a city within a city. Everything it needed to function was on site. As well as the bag room and killing floor, there were chemists, shipping clerks, tinsmiths, plumbers, engineers, vets and accountants. There was a fire truck and a steam train. Online I found a couple of aerial pictures taken in the 1920s. In them, Islington spilled out onto the land around it, building after building, rows of chimneys. It was something out of an L.S. Lowry painting, a satanic mill. 'It was a big affair, a monstrous affair,' said Uncle Dale. 'There were tunnels and Christ knows what.' But an industrial landscape is still a landscape; as well as its killing sheds and freezing rooms, this one even had a manmade lake – the water used to cool ammonia condensers.

Islington was on that roll-call of closures. They're building a business park where it used to be, uncovering pits of buried carcasses in the process. My grandfather retired not long before it closed, but Mum told me he'd been shocked by the news. My uncle managed to stay working for a while longer, as the bag room remained open to supply those works that remained. He would later go into business himself using some of the same skills. He worked out of his garage repairing the chain-link gloves worn by butchers. Both men were lucky, escaping early or finding late-career lifeboats. For others, the end of the local freezing works meant the dole. Sometimes it meant despair. In Pātea, the churches held weekly prayer meetings after the works closed. Jacq Dwyer told me the town took a generation to recover. There were still empty sections where houses had been jacked up and shifted away.

*

There was once a freezing works down the road from where I live in the Wairarapa: Waingawa. Before it closed in 1989, it was the biggest employer in the region, hiring seven hundred people during the killing season. A man named Marshall Coley was the union president at the time, and was part of a welfare group that tried to soften the blow of closure. They'd had a community, he told me. They had sports teams. In fact, there was a national games, a sort of freezing workers' Olympics, that ran from the early 70s to the late 80s. Coley said that after the closure he helped relocate people to places where they might find work. Although, not everyone had somewhere to go. He learned of a former worker who had been leaving his house at six o'clock every morning, driving out into the country where he could sit in his car and read a book. He didn't want his neighbours to know he'd been made redundant, Coley said.

Their old workplace lingered, abandoned for years. But by the time I moved here it had been demolished. A row of oaks on a side road is all that remains. They were planted by the managers on what was once the road to the works. I'd driven past them many times, admiring the glade their sturdy frames made. Then I learned about the works, and when I see them now I think of a car parked on a lonely road, the tick of a dashboard clock, a man reading a book.

You might say we're better off with fewer freezing works. This was brutal, unpleasant work. I know I'd last a solid two minutes in one – I get woozy at the sight of blood. But I've always been drawn to the past, never been able to think clearly about the future. My neck is cricked, looking back. Almost twenty years into a new century, and here I am still wondering about that old New Zealand of 'full employment' and six o'clock swills. It was a place that was busily being dismantled in the years I learnt to read. Unknowable then for me, except as the setting for my grandfather's stories. And yet in many ways, he never belonged either. He didn't socialise at 'the Swamp' – the pub where freezing workers congregated, and when he was conscripted into the army (he missed combat due to an untreatable set of bunions) he preferred to spend his evenings at needlepoint by numbers rather than boozing with his fellow soldiers. Mine is the definition of misplaced nostalgia. It was him I missed. All I really knew of the works was that he'd been there. In the memories I hold he is spooling out his tape measure, leaning towards a piece of wood with the stub of a carpenter's pencil, moving slowly, without coming to a stop. When he did finally wind up in a rest home without tools to hold or a garden to tend, it was clear from the start he wouldn't be there long. He sat in his room, like that man in his car, waiting.

My grandfather was important to me. 'The works' was a place important to him. Some part of me can't help but feel those words like a sunset still.

# Grassroots Elvis

Elvis was Māori. He was Pākehā. He was young. He was usually fairly old. He was drunk, possibly, or maybe just feeling nervy. He was blind, helped to his cane when stepping off the stage. He looked remarkably like Walter Matthau, like Nick Cave, like Neil Diamond, sometimes even like Elvis. He was us, New Zealand, on a Friday night out at the Upper Hutt Cosmopolitan Club.

There were lights and red curtains. Each letter of 'ELVIS' took its turn to flash bright onstage, and on my table a small plastic puck glowed to show that my Cossie Burger was ready. These were the heats of Elvis Down Under, and eight Elvises (Elvi?) would be chosen for a final. It was, the compère said, 'grassroots Elvis' – two words that still bounce together in my head. He was an Elvis himself, an Aussie in a cerise shirt. Before the show started, he gathered the sixteen competitors together for a briefing, setting out the fundamentals in a corner of the Cossie Club function room. The voice is only 40 per cent of it, he said, and your songs better match the era of your costume.

The latter meant that the good-time hits of early Elvis,

'Hound Dog' and 'Jailhouse Rock', barely got a look in. These were almost all the Elvis of the Vegas years, the days of jumpsuits and drugs and that famous sandwich. The first did a reasonable job, wearing a terrific powder-blue suit. The second was too small for his, he was lost in it; it resembled a rhinestoned onesie. But his 'Love Me Tender' was a beautiful thing, a highlight. And from then I lost track. They were everywhere. Elvis would leave the stage as Elvis walked on, introduced by Elvis, while yet another ducked past on his way to the bar. There were a few who forgot their words, and a few real standouts, including one of two who did Hawaiian Elvis. Yes, they sounded good, but it was their ease, their comfort on stage that was their greatest strength. They could karate chop and stab at the air with the mic and still look cool. Aussie Elvis was right: the voice was less than half of it.

The last time I was here another crowd had come to commune with the dead. It was the day of the Upper Hutt Psychic Fair. There were tarot readers, healers and spirit mediums, and a lady who could communicate psychically with pets, alive or dead – all she needed was a photograph. Elvis Down Under was another mass séance. It operated on a similar principle – both parties meeting each other halfway – but seemed more honest to me. 'The more you drink the more I look like Elvis,' said one impersonator. We had come here aware of the illusion and were now all working together to transcend it, channelling another time, a past youth, a shared joy, or simply the apogee of entertainment – lights and lamé and soul-infused rock'n'roll. 'Tomorrow they'll do the gospel songs, and I'll be here crying,' one lady told us. Wasn't Elvis himself an impersonator in those final, bloated days – putting on the act so we might still have all of those things?

*

When Brendon Chase took the stage, the mood changed. New Zealand's top Elvis impersonator, he wasn't competing but was there to cap off the night. I realised I had walked past him earlier, just another Elvis, I had thought, maybe a bit more tanned – but on stage he had an easy writhe and that effortless deep voice. His suit was meticulously embroidered with a giant peacock. He strolled through the crowd, his hips rolling like a man at sea, stepping across tables to sing 'Never Been to Spain', a soft rock hit by Three Dog Night later made swaggering and altogether cooler by the King.

After Chase, the finalists would be announced, and we'd be thrown back into the world of artifice, admitting that some were more real than others. But I had a train to catch, and when I made my exit he was still going, still surrounded by women wanting his sweat-drenched scarves, the past still ours to relive. I left the building before Elvis. The better ending.

# Living Springs

My education began with a kindly, elderly lady named Grimshaw, who I remember for the pendulous necklaces she wore and which hung, noose-like, near my own neck whenever she leaned in to inspect my work. I can recall once having to stay perfectly still when, having hooked me, Mrs Grimshaw rose unaware she was inflicting a garrotting. But on reflection, I think this is a case of one of my many imaginings entering the memory as fact. What is certain is that she spent a lot of time looking at my work. My letters would occasionally double back on each other or roll about drunkenly on the lines of my book. Once when my mother came to pick me up, I proudly chalked what I believed to be a question mark on the board and turned to see, from her expression, that it made as much sense to her as a Viking rune. Dyslexia was suspected, and Mrs Grimshaw took it upon herself to help. She held me back after school for tuition, employing methods that time has rendered questionable. We spent many of these afternoons trying to read books upside down. But then maybe these techniques worked, or maybe I grew out of it, because over the years my letters began to right themselves and gradually they stood to attention. I wrote sentences recognisable as English. What didn't change was the daydreaming. I was a shy, moony boy, always wandering in a fog of half ideas. There was that notion of the necklaces for example, or my belief that I was a gymnastics prodigy. This one came about after I alone was asked to join older pupils in a weekly gymnastics class (maybe this is too generous – it was a half an hour of roly-polying across the school hall floor). What I didn't notice, and had to be told much later, was that this was in fact another attempt, in that era of Brain Gym, at sparking my sluggish mind into action.

This school was beside a river, not far from the base of Christchurch's Port Hills. A collection of buildings that began with a solid old classroom from before the war, but was mostly the more usual, flimsy prefabs with wire glass in the doors and holey tiles in the ceiling. From Mrs Grimshaw, I next went to Miss Hoy and then to Mrs Pascoe, working my way through those classrooms, learning things, probably. Very few of the memories I have from these early years are of class. Instead I recall being overcome by the desire to throw a boy's shoes into the murky space beneath a storeroom while he queued to use the long jump pit, and then cowering in fear when he caught up with me days later and threatened a beating. A happy ending of sorts would come when this storeroom was torched by an arsonist one Saturday, removing the prompt for this unpleasant memory. I also remember the intimate and unaffected friendship of those years, something not repeated since, when, with me the last to learn to tie my shoes, we might stop our games so a friend could tie them for me. And I remember the way we spent our lunch breaks, sticking our arms out, making a droning sound, the pitch higher for a dive, so we could recreate the Battle of Britain on the chewed-up grass in front of Room Four. More accurately, we could recreate the Battle of Britain as depicted in a TV show we watched religiously, *Piece of Cake*. My arms became wings, my smooth upper lip sprouted a tidy moustache. I swelled with stoic British heroism. Adult life was like that, I hoped, even as I feared and somehow knew it was closer to a show that my mother watched and which I sometimes caught glimpses of: *Taxi*. A world where people had grey or thinning hair and coarse, unheroic features. People whose lives contained none of the things I dreamed of, no adventure, no war. The wistful jazz flute of its theme song still feels to me like the distillation of a Sunday afternoon in autumn, an unsatisfactory work week approaching. The only thing for it was to drone louder, make the pow-pow of guns, and get ready to bail out, let the silk of the parachute billow up above, so I might float back down to the grass, ready to take off and confront my foe once again, the battle never ending, death never coming.

My feelings on *Taxi* spoke to a broader fear, one that grabbed me each year as summer approached, and with it the end of class and the eventual need to begin all over again with another teacher. It's common to think of kids as natural optimists. So much of the future lies before them; they live facing a tangerine horizon. But to me, it was distressing to think about the years ahead. Each movement through the strata of standards and forms came with a whole new set of expectations about who you would be, and what you should know, until eventually you got to high school, the most terrifying and unforgiving place of all. A big part of this worry was my inability to keep up, especially with maths. It felt that there were things we were expected to know without them ever being taught. When I arrived in Standard Three, our teacher, a dynamic young man with spiky hair and track pants, had us recite our times tables. When were we supposed to have learnt those? And yet it seemed others had. They joined him in a chorus while I mumbled through the hard ones, speaking up only for the easiest three: the twos, the fives and the tens. Maybe I had daydreamed through that lesson? This was possible. My daydreaming had evolved over the years, gradually moving from a reality-blurring fog to something more specific – single thoughts that would go on for too long, temporarily obliterating the world around me. Looking out the window, I might begin to wonder how I would go about outfitting a ship to explore the Bermuda Triangle and, when I next looked back to class, would discover that we had finished fractions for the day.

A similar change happened in our play. It went from those unfocused games, from sticking our arms out to make wings, to games with strict rules like tag, and later to sports. Our soccer matches were medieval battles: teams indistinguishable, a melee on a muddy field. Most often though we played cricket. From around the age of nine or ten, I became a member of a group of boys who played in the back field, playing over every lunch, morning and afternoon break, abandoning our books at the first peal of the bell to run for the birch tree we used as stumps. Once, forgetting something, I had to return to class on one of these breaks and found, in the evidence of our hurrying away, an eerie absence, a *Marie Celeste* of dropped pens and chairs left askew, the strangeness of all this added to by someone in an adjoining room endlessly drilling 'Heart and Soul' on the piano. I rushed back out to the field.

Even there, while fielding, I'd sometimes find myself emerging from my thoughts to realise that I hadn't paid attention to the game for a dangerously long time and, looking about to reorient myself, would spy the ball in the air above my head. I cupped my hands, staggered back and forth ready to catch it, only to see it loop and fly away, just a bird.

Still, something did pierce these imaginings, because it was in those cricketing years that I can trace the beginnings of one of the more important lessons I learnt from school – again not from the classroom, at least not just, but from the playground and the streets too. Our school was in an affluent neighbourhood, surrounded by well-tended homes and yards with established trees and late-model cars. These homes were what our teachers meant when they said 'house'. I knew that, and I became attuned to difference, capable of spotting whose shoes were from Hannahs (best), Dowsons (worse, and the source of my own battered sneakers) or the Warehouse (worst). I knew who had spent time at Glenelg Health Camp, where kids went when there was trouble at home, and I knew who lived on Kowhai Terrace, a street of state houses just over the river, presumably built in the name of pepper potting, the experiment of scattering them among the well-to-do to prompt integration. In some ways this experiment worked: we went to school with both the children of a brain surgeon and the children of Cambodian refugees. But in other ways it failed, and this failure was the doing of kids like me. Just to say the name Kowhai Terrace was to bring up all the associations that went with that street, the poverty of junked cars and the same old clothes worn every day, vague ideas of crime and people up to no good.

From here, I can see that cricket fed my desire for sameness. Why else would you play it? Unless you were batting, it was a deeply boring game. By playing, though, I became indistinguishable from those other boys, just another set of skinny limbs and floppy hair, desperately chasing a tennis ball. We had this common interest and it made even a daydreamer like me feel serious and important. Adults played these games. At home, a poster of the Canterbury team, twelve unsmiling men in nylon, hung on my bedroom wall. Together, my fellow cricketers and I talked about the need to rough the ball on our pants before attempting spin, and the importance of breaking in a bat before its first use. Some laid their bats out on the scuffed grass, explaining why their brand was best. You could only buy GM they said, only Kookaburra, only Grey-Nicolls. Their dads had said so, and nothing was more definitive than the words of a dad.

Cricket eventually took me to Kowhai Terrace. One of my fellow players lived there and invited me to his house for an after-school game. Jeffrey was the English name he went by – it was his parents who were Cambodian refugees – and when I arrived, we were joined by another boy from school, Simon, who lived on that street with his mother and brother, and who was bullied by our classmates. I never took part in this bullying but I never spoke out against it either, instead quietly watching as others chased him around the back field, trying to figure out what made him such a target. I'm sure Kowhai Terrace was part of it, the name bringing its whiff of poverty, of difference. Of course, Jeffrey was different too, but in a way that held a fascination. He told us stories about his parents fleeing Cambodia, and about them once owning a monkey. We didn't think of his life as lacking. And just as importantly, he was outgoing, he had spunk. He quickly became popular and it surprised me to discover that he and Simon hung out together, not friends maybe but comrades.

Jeffrey asked me to bring a cricket bat that day. Neither he nor Simon owned one. I ummed and ahhed, but finally did bring mine, a beautiful object that my grandfather had made. After watching those bat line-ups enviously, desperate to take part, I had petitioned Mum. As with most of my wants, word had gone back to my grandparents. My grandfather went out to his shed and turned a handle on a piece of old kauri. He planed the face and back, sanded it down till it glowed like a gold ingot and, where the logo would go, inscribed 'John' with a hot poker. I feigned gratitude. Bats needed to be new. You could only buy GM, only Kookaburra, only Grey-Nicolls. Those dads had spoken.

Simon sniggered when I revealed this homemade bat. More than anyone, he knew the order of things. 'Ha! This isn't a real one,' he said.

I cringed, and for a moment I wanted to remind him of the horrible things the bullies had called him.

Jeffrey reached for the bat. 'Shut up,' he said quietly. 'It's cool.' He ran a finger over the inscription.

Simon went quiet, and the three of us took our places: batter, bowler, fielder. The bare minimum for a game. We played on. We ran up and down Jeffrey's backyard until the light began to dim.

That was the only time I showed that bat to someone else. I had brought it knowing that it would be safe there at Kowhai Terrace. The truth was I had much in common with those two, maybe more than I did with the friends who lived close to school in well-tended homes. Like Simon, it was just me, mum and my brother at home. Our house was several blocks away from the school, in another suburb again, and on a narrow street of houses badly in need of a paint. Across the road lived an old man who sat on his front step to clip his toenails and watch his brother leave for the pub each day. There was another school much closer to us, but it was for rough kids, Mum said, and so we walked an extra fifteen minutes to ours and did our best to fit in with the others there and to notice who came from Kowhai Terrace. Their presence was a reassurance, marking the outer boundary of our world, allowing me to feel closer to the centre.

Jeffrey visited me at my house once. I don't remember what we did, but cricket is a safe guess. I do know that when it came time for him to leave, Mum noticed he wasn't wearing enough clothes for the chill of an early evening in autumn and gave him a windbreaker that had been hanging unwanted in my wardrobe. It was secondhand, with the logo of a local rugby league club across the back. He admired it, and from then on I often saw him wearing it at school, half-zipped like James Dean's jacket. Although I'd never worn it myself, I began to regret that Mum had given it away. On him it looked cool. He wore it with his usual confidence, a sleight of hand that distracted from his difference. This was a trick I admired but couldn't emulate. Fumbling and hiding were my ways of getting by. I kept my bat to myself. I didn't risk wearing that old windbreaker. And I listened carefully to others and took their cue, methods not available to Jeffrey or Simon, their difference too marked.

I was, in other words, a follower. Never a leader, never a rebel. When do you first realise that about yourself? I don't think I knew it then, even as it guided almost everything I did: cricket of course, but also, for one brief period, membership of the school choir. A friend suggested joining and I agreed even though it went against everything I knew. I hated singing, and the choir practised during lunchbreak, our single, sacred half hour of free time. Even worse, it was led by Mr

Watson. My fear of him was part of that more general fear of the years ahead. He taught Form Twos, the oldest children at our school, and they seemed so large, so impossibly adult. We steered well clear, and it was my belief that only someone more or at least equally terrifying could teach them. Mr Watson certainly had a presence. He was recognisable from afar, a bald and wiry Englishman whose eyes were made large by the same square, plastic glasses that David Lange wore throughout his prime ministership. Each morning, he arrived in a green Mini, wearing, no matter the weather, a kind of safari get-up: shorts and shirt of the same pale beige. Well before choir, we had been introduced to him as a maestro of sorts, when during assemblies we were all made to sing 'Surfin' USA' to his accompaniment on the school keyboard (from that point on, I have carried the words 'huarache sandals' in my head, without ever quite knowing what they meant). These sightings were enough for me to believe that Mr Watson was a strict and rigid man, and yet I did what others did and when one of my good friends, a cricketer and a soccer player named Michael, went to Mr Watson's choir, I followed. One lunch per week would be spent in dry, hot rooms while games went on outside. Mr Watson spoke at us all with urgency as we sang, waving his hands in a way that was supposed to convey some instruction. Wary of getting this wrong, I made sure my voice wasn't loud enough to be heard, just a faint echo that blended into the rest. Eventually though, we couldn't face another lunchbreak cooped up with the Beach Boys and when it came time for choir we simply carried on as if we'd never joined and played cricket instead. I say we, but of course this was not my decision. Just as I had followed my friends into choir, so I followed them out.

The next day, our teacher had us cleaning the classroom, picking up all the minute pieces of torn paper that we managed to produce in our lessons, when Mr Watson entered and summoned me, Michael and another chorister. We followed him into the computer room adjoining our class, the final resting place for two beige PCs, and there he berated us. He didn't quite yell, but it was close enough, a terse, angry lecture. 'You can't just not turn up to things because you don't feel like it,' he said after someone explained why we'd skipped rehearsals. In my memory this all went on for an hour, so it was probably a good ten minutes. Mr Watson took his time telling us all off as a group, then as individuals, before turning back to the group as a whole. It was when he was talking to one of the others that I noticed a silhouette at the window in the computer room door. The textured glass meant this person was indistinct, but I recognised Zara, a classmate of ours who was infamous for eating Blu-Tack as if it were bubblegum. She loved the stuff. Someone once saw her peel a trodden piece off the carpet and pop it in her mouth. Her silhouette caught Mr Watson's attention too, and there followed a slow five seconds in which we all turned to the window to see her hazy shape look to the right and then the left, making sure she had no witness, before peeling back the corner of a notice stuck to that window. She pulled off one of the dobs of Blu-Tack that held it in place and let the picture fall loosely back to the glass before hurrying away. Mr Watson frowned. He seemed to consider saying something, but instead turned back to us to carry on his lecture. Michael whispered to me. 'She's going to eat it,' he said. It was then that I exploded. I snorted and hissed and writhed, and all of my attempts at containing my laughter only made it more of a performance.

'Get out!' Mr Watson said. 'Go outside and wait.'

I exited the computer room and passed my classmates. I had time to envy their busy, innocent tidying before walking down the long linoleumed hallway lined with backpacks to stand by the door. I was terrified of course, but this terror came to me as the calm of the condemned man. Time stopped. I sank beneath the surface of the earth. 'What are you waiting for?' asked some kid returning from the dental clinic.

'Mr Watson is going to tell me off,' I said matter-of-factly.

He pulled a face, thinking me stoic, not seeing that my terror was too big for panic, before heading on back to class.

Eventually, I heard Mr Watson's steps on the lino. He emerged from the shadows of that corridor and stood over me, arms akimbo. I waited for his telling-off. But he was calm now.

'You couldn't help yourself, could you?' he said, and this question came, not as an accusation but simply as recognition. I believed, in that moment, that he knew something, understood something I didn't. Maybe he knew I had never wanted to join his choir, nor wanted to quit, that I had simply been carried along all the way to that spot, where I stood outside, scared of being told off, while class went on without me.

'No,' I said.

'I thought that was the case.' He told me to head back to class, our roles intact, the stern teacher, the timid boy, without either of us needing to say any more.

Mr Watson would remain a constant figure, a part of many memories of those days, at school camp for instance, an event that loomed large on the calendar. Weeks out we were given a list of the clothes and equipment we would need, and I seized on this, obsessive as usual about having the right things, the same things as everyone else. Mum and I traipsed around the Warehouse looking for cheap gumboots, and I begged her to buy three overpriced boxes of scroggin off the Scouts, taken in by the school's description of it as outdoors food. I believe that

Mr Watson was behind this. Although yet to be my teacher, he was regarded as the school's resident outdoorsman as well as pianist, and saw camps as justification to spend hours of class time on survival training. We once sat puzzled, watching him thread a rope through his crotch so he could demonstrate how to belay without a harness.

His lessons were of zero use at our first camp, held at a place called Living Springs. We were bused most of the way there from school and then walked a few kilometres through bush and farmland. I walked near another teacher, Miss Duggan, and someone's mother who was there as a parent helper. The fields were the same parched beige as Mr Watson's shorts, and the moments when we entered the gloom of the bush were like a cool drink. At one point in our hike, a girl from the class above mine came running over.

'Miss Duggan,' she said in a panic, and told how she'd heard that a boy named David had 'vodka and alcohol' in his bag. David was someone else I associated with Kowhai Terrace, although I didn't know him as well as Jeffrey and Simon. He was one of those terrifying Form Twos, maybe the most terrifying. He got into fights and always seemed in need of a wash, and most frighteningly of all, he didn't seem to give a shit. He didn't try and fail to join in, like Simon, and he didn't have Jeffrey's charm. Instead he was apart from the rest of us, serious and grown up.

'Hmm,' Miss Duggan said at the suggestion that he might be smuggling booze. She looked down the track and narrowed her eyes like a gunfighter. 'I'll look into it.'

The girl walked away, and Miss Duggan turned to the parent helper. 'I could do with some of that right now!' she said.

They both chortled and we carried on to camp.

We would go on one other walk on that camp, but again Mr Watson's lessons went untested. This one was led by one of the Christians that ran the place, an older, bearded man of the bush. He told us a story from his childhood about squeezing wood pigeons to make them give up their berries. A bullshit artist I now suspect, but as a boy I had no filter for the weird self-aggrandisement that some adults were prone to around kids. I was impressed when he told us that not once in his forty-something years had he ever been on a benefit. It seemed unbelievable to me – Mum had needed to get the dole from time to time, and jobs were elusive things, I thought; you held them the way you might grip a wet cake of soap. But when I came home and told her, she didn't share my astonishment. 'Lots of people could say that,' she said abruptly, offended. '. . . Your Uncle Dale.'

That evening, we slept six to a bunkroom. I was up top and anxious about falling out. I'd heard a horror story about someone doing that and biting their own lips off. But trouble came from beyond the room, a sudden bustle outside. Loud voices. Teachers sounding serious. The next day the rumour spread. David, Luke and some of the older boys had been sent home. I was desperate to know exactly what had happened. I sought out a boy named Craig who sat, before an audience, at a round table in the camp dining room.

'You want to know why David was sent home?' he said. 'I can tell you why.'

I nodded for him to hurry up, and he laid his hands very gently on the table. He spoke slowly. 'David,' he said, 'brought cocaine to camp.'

Of course, it was the vodka. David had brought a bottle of Coca-Cola laced with booze and stashed it in his bag. This would be later confirmed at a serious talk given to us all by Mr Watson, who spoke quietly, his eyes sad behind his thick lenses. Later, I would come to learn that David was the mysterious piano player I had once heard during lunch and that it was with Mr Watson's encouragement and tuition that he spent his breaks practising 'Heart and Soul'. Now he'd been turfed out of camp. No doubt those Christians wanted him gone.

David's wasn't the only scandal at that camp. There was a second incident which again caused our teachers to go about with grave faces. This time, we were all summoned. We went one by one to a room. 'What's it about?'

'Something with the toilets.'

When it came my turn, I stepped into the room, where a man with a gingery beard sat, waiting.

He smiled. 'John, I want you to tell me the truth about something,' he said. 'You won't be in trouble if you tell the truth.'

I nodded. I understood.

That morning, I had been gathered with my friends, all in a hurry to go somewhere, when I felt the urgent need of the toilet. Somehow, my mind elsewhere yet again, too shy to announce my need to go, I held on until it was far too late. When I finally burst into the stall, I was in a hopeless state, my pants fouled. Even so I sat there for ten minutes, not sure what to do. I heard friends outside. 'Where is he?'

'In the toilet.'

'Still?'

Finally, I took my underpants off and, mindful not to block the toilet, I threw them into a corner.

Now the smiling man looked me in the eye. In a kindly tone, he asked, 'Do you know anything about what happened in the toilets?'

'No,' I said.

He thanked me and I left the room to get the next kid for questioning. I never owned up, not to him or anyone else, convinced for so long that I had committed the worst possible crime, so unmentionable that eventually I buried it completely. Only now do I realise it's safe to recall this incident. No teacher is coming to track me down. No one is going to humiliate me in a classroom. I see too that even had I been caught back then, I would have been let off with, at worst, a stern talking to, the teachers recognising my actions, as Mr Watson once had, as a childish mistake. My sort of mistake. David's crime, on the other hand, was flagrant. He'd told people about his intentions on day one. There was talk of him being expelled, but I doubt it fazed him. He didn't seem to care about the things we were told to care about. He was the tough kid, the rough kid. Parents would worry if their children said his name, and perhaps they tutted about his home. There was no chance of him not being an outsider at that school. At least, it seems to me, he'd chosen the reason why.

What I have here is, to some degree, a catalogue of worries which came to nothing. On camp and on so many other occasions, the consequences I expected passed me by, kept passing me by. I was a daydreamer. I was hopeless at maths. These things didn't change, and yet I still made it through each new year of class, made it all the way through high school, university even, right up to my working life, the vantage point from where I might look smugly back, write a letter to my younger self. It all comes right in the end, I could say. No one does division in their head anyway! Except that I suspect it's him who should be writing to me. 'Those emotions were real when we felt them,' Graham Greene once wrote, and I always liked this, found it easy to agree, because those emotions remain real still. Yes, the specific fears are gone, and there's a kind of nostalgia to be had in recalling this, in thinking of how often time proved my fears false, but the worries behind them never really went away. I still find myself slipping into daydreams in meeting rooms, still anxious to be the same and fearful of what comes ahead, wringing my hands at each new job and then, when the job has begun, at each new task or problem, even as each time I make it through, those worries never realised. In theory, knowing all this should give me some power, an ability to break this pattern, but that seems as likely as forgetting reading or writing or my rudimentary maths. I don't know whether these fears were lessons I learnt in childhood or qualities drawn out and made distinct over those years, but either way they linger. An education never ends.

My last year at that school meant I was finally one of those grown-up, miniature adults I had watched all those years earlier: a Form Two. But, of course, any change had come too gradually for me to notice, and by then I could only see how far I still was from adulthood. Occasionally I glimpsed high-schoolers on the street, old in their uniforms, and somehow unwholesome I thought too, with their acne and insouciance. They would be wheeling their bikes back from school, swearing to each other, smirking at the sight of a little boy like me lugging a too-big backpack.

It was in that year too that, after all those encounters, I finally had Mr Watson as my teacher. The choir incident was long forgotten, and like Mrs Grimshaw he was mostly encouraging, doing what he knew to prepare us for the years ahead. He introduced our lesson on speeches by acknowledging the whole thing was a drag, but then told a story about him drifting apart from a good friend because, scared of public speaking, he had refused to be best man at his wedding. The story has stayed with me, a reminder not to always fall back on my own innate shyness. But by far the most memorable of his preparations was a weekly hour or so of sex education that we were given in our final months there. It wasn't called quite that – I forget the èxact title, but it centred on the mechanics of puberty and Mr Watson took a fairly wide brief. Girls were sent elsewhere to have these lessons from one of the female teachers, and so it was him and a dozen or so prepubescent boys. He taught with the same gusto he brought to compasses and belaying. This was another set of survival skills. Recognising the combination of curiosity and embarrassment in the room, he invited us to anonymously submit any questions we had, anything at all. He then read them out to us all and did his best to provide answers. At least half of these questions were facetious, planted for our entertainment, but still he spoke to them earnestly, smiling only gently in recognition of the fact that throughout we were all howling, aggressive in our laughter, desperately clinging to childhood at the very moment we were being told of its dying days. 'When I walk ...' he read, his accent proper, his eyes narrowed at wild handwriting. 'My . . . pubs . . . tickle my bum.'

'Pubes,' shouted a boy from the back of the class. 'It says pubes.'

Again, we howled. Looking around me, I saw everyone was together in this, the rich boys and the poor, the cool and the wretched. We were all the same in our fear, and I was, for that brief moment, as happy as I had been at any time in all my years at that school.

A few months later I would start high school.

# The House that Norm Built

When Norman Kirk died, the president of Tanzania wept. In China, Zhou Enlai bowed three times to his photograph. He had been prime minister for just under two years, long enough to introduce the DPB, to send a Navy frigate to protest French nuclear testing in the Pacific, and to grow our ties, not with England or America, but with Asia, the Pacific and the developing world. We mourned here too, of course. National Radio played sombre music, Denis Glover and C.K. Stead wrote poems (Stead's is better) and people lined the streets. Although not me. I was born nine years later and my first encounter with the man was a book – just the spine to be exact. Margaret Hayward's *Diary of the Kirk Years* sat on a shelf near my father's dining table and, during meals, the bold white lettering of the title with its koru-like serifs on those two *k*s was a tractor beam to my eye. It was a disappointment, each time I found myself looking at it, to remember that it was about politics. And yet, seeing that book prominent among the novels and gardening guides for all those years meant I always carried the idea that Kirk was important. I'd read on or listen if his name came up, just as you do at any mention of someone you know, however faintly. A copy of that book sits on my own shelves now.

There's a picture of Kirk in which he's unrecognisable, just a tiny figure clinging to the top of a dairy factory chimney – it must have been at least four storeys high. He was painting it, a job he did for extra cash while he worked at the factory as a boiler operator. His had been a Depression-era childhood: grim (the family once ate onions for days on end, the only thing they could successfully grow) and short; he'd left school at age thirteen for a series of tough and grimy jobs, mixing roof paint out of boiling pitch and asbestos, cleaning locomotives by rubbing them down with grit and animal fat, and shovelling coal on the Devonport Ferry. He was twenty-one when he got to Katikati, and was already married to Ruth, his first girlfriend, with a son and another child on the way. They lived in a hut provided by the company, and Kirk spent his evenings fighting off the rats that nibbled the softboard walls. 'It was a problem and we dealt with it,' he later told interviewer David Frost, speaking with a curious whistle in his exhale and declining to say much more. The rats had already become part of the Kirk mythology by then, made famous by a biography rushed out for his election campaign, which described him barging into a directors' meeting and throwing a ripe, dead rat on the table, demanding they do something about it. They replaced the lining of the hut with a rat-proof hardboard. Even so, the Kirks moved on to look for a more permanent home. They went south to Kaiapoi, a town just out of Christchurch, so close now that it's like another suburb, albeit one kept at arm's length by the motorway. Cheap property was the appeal. Kirk bought a section and, unable to afford a builder, he took on the job himself. He biked to the site between shifts at Christchurch's Firestone tyre factory, balancing timber on his handlebars, and built a concrete-clad rectangle: a single-storey home with a flat roof that leaked a little.

I've always found this house fascinating, our version of the old American myth of log cabin to White House. Not hand-hewn but rough-cast, a bit leaky, a bit cold – an unremarkable chunk of post-war architecture. I was especially taken by a single sentence I came across: 'He cast the cinderblocks himself.' I haven't been able to find this sentence again. Maybe I'd imagined it in this particular form, but that's how I remembered it, and I loved it as something that felt particular to New Zealand: aiming for big things, the almost biblical cadence of 'cast', only to fall flat on that most prosaic of building materials, the cinderblock.

Kirk made those blocks from concrete mixed to his own recipe: a combination of cement, sand, and coke grease that he'd scavenged from Firestone. But you need water for concrete too, and so the first thing he did was sink a well by driving a steel pipe 70 feet into the ground. He and his father made a mould and into this they poured the concrete, producing over a thousand blocks, which he laid around a native timber frame. The whole thing was then topped with a flat roof of Malthoid, a tar-soaked felt that was cheaper than iron and that would need regular patching to keep the rain out.

With the help of my partner's grandparents, who live in Kaiapoi, I found this house – a solid single-storey home on a flat street of solid single-storey homes, remarkable only for its plainness. There's nothing to tell you it was ever Kirk's, no plaque or signs. A burly, cheery Englishman named Philip Dobb lives there now with his partner and their three cats. We chatted in a lounge out the back, sitting on his leather sofa, a packet of tobacco and all the fixings by his side. 'He couldn't use a tape measure,' Dobb said. There was a 30 to 40-millimetre difference between the top of the door and bottom. 'All the floor joists were just sort of thrown in place.' There was no design to them. He was scathing too of Kirk's blocks – you could poke a screwdriver right through them – but did concede that the timber frame was more than strong enough.

Dobb had bought the house off a mate – they'd shaken on the deal at the pub – after helping the man insulate and rewire. He was an electrical engineer and had since put in a heat pump and double glazing. 'It would have been freezing back in the day,' he said. He'd also installed a rotating solar panel out back for hot water, and built a new kitchen. It seemed mid-DIY when I turned up. Years before that someone had replaced the Malthoid with a hipped iron roof, and in the 70s they'd added the room that Dobb and I sat in. Every so often he gets a letter from Heritage New Zealand saying the house 'is still a heritage whatever', but he reckoned it's near the bottom of their list. It was like the story of the old, old axe, the handle and head replaced many times over. The house that Norm built was in there somewhere, but you needed to squint to see it.

Kirk was living in this homemade home when he started his political career in earnest. He became involved in the local branch of the Labour party, and ran, successfully, for the Kaiapoi mayoralty. He was the youngest mayor in the country at thirty and he held the job while still working at Firestone. His practical nous stood out. His council built a modern sewerage system, as well as roads, footpaths and parks. Kirk learnt as he went, reading up on politics and, appropriately, introducing an adult education programme.* His success led Labour to shoulder-tap him to run, unsuccessfully, for MP of Hurunui, and then for Lyttelton, a swing seat he would make theirs. From there he raced through the ranks, becoming party president in 1964 and leader in 65. He was young (Walter Nash had only recently retired as Labour leader at age eighty), he was hardworking, and he could be ruthless. Ad man Bob Harvey recalled a meeting where Kirk told him he'd 'stomp on any bastard' that got in his way.

Harvey would help with what was most likely the first makeover in our political history. Kirk grew out his short back and sides hairdo to something more suitably flowing for the late 1960s. He lost weight and bought better suits. In 1972, transformed, he went up against Jack Marshall, the charisma-lite National leader who had become prime minister when the immensely popular Keith Holyoake stepped down. The election was a landslide.

After all Kirk went through to find a home for his family, it's no great surprise that housing was a theme of his political life, from the mayoralty onwards. His government expanded state housing and introduced policies for accessible loans, a crackdown on property speculation, rent caps and a scheme to rent land out cheaply for hippie communes (it was the 70s, after all). And in this, there's a case for Kirk's relevance. Home ownership has become elusive again, and a generational debate rages on the topic: baby boomers are accused of squeezing the young – the millennials – out of the property market, while

* Libraries in the region still hold a Norman Kirk Collection comprised entirely of DIY manuals. Titles include *The Complete Book of Home Improvement* by Mike Lawrence and *Paths, Steps & Patios for the Garden: Including 16 Easy-to-Build Projects* by Alan Bridgewater.

millennials are accused of not working hard enough or of frittering away what might otherwise be their house deposit. Avocados, the most-cited symbol of millennial profligacy, are lobbed like hand grenades in this generational war. Kirk had heard that complaint, that the young expected too much. 'So they should,' he said. 'I started where my father left off, he started where his father left off. And my children ought to start at a better point than I did. That's what we believe in if we believe in progress.'

Kaiapoi hadn't been the first place Kirk looked to build his house. He had considered the cheap quarter-acre sections to be had in the Christchurch suburb of Hornby, but was put off the area by the chemical works nearby. I smiled when I came across this, because my grandparents had one of those Hornby sections, a long garden that began with roses and included the garage my grandfather built and an enormous vegetable patch. Like Kirk, my grandfather left school at thirteen and laboured, in his case on farms and on wharfs, before learning a trade. This part of Kirk's story was familiar to me. It's probably what got me into the car and driving out to Kaiapoi. Even though I'm (only just) a millennial myself, those generational debates never really interested me. The system is broken I agree, but I'm sure that the wealth that many of those baby boomers are amassing from property will eventually make its way to their millennial children. And there are boomers left out as well; they count among the renters and the poor buggers sleeping in cars. In my mother's case, the boomer I know best, it was only a near thing that she, a single parent of two boys, was able to buy her house. I don't see her making hay off the soaring price of property anytime soon.

In our eagerness to lay fault it feels like we've forgotten that class is still at play, that people are losing for reasons other than their birthdate. It's something we don't talk about anymore, maybe not since Kirk's day. But, apart from Mike Moore's brief stint in the job, he was our last working-class prime minister, his house literally concrete proof of this status – not a villa or the sort of place that gets to become charming or quaint with time, but a simple three-bedroom box, just as my grandparents' home was. I'm told they liked Kirk even though they were generally uninterested in politics and distrustful of politicians as being 'all jaw'. The reason they liked him, I'm sure, was his pre-political life. He'd been through the things they had, lived a life they could recognise before taking office and telling the French to back off, pulling us out of Vietnam and giving pensioners a Christmas bonus. That background, still visible in that old house, showed that those values don't have to be, as they're often portrayed, the preserve of the educated and the urban. It told a story about the way we like to think of ourselves, the way I like to think of my grandparents – as citizens of a country where a particular sort of decency could be innate.

Margaret Hayward worked for Kirk, but long before that she was his neighbour. She grew up next door and watched him build his house. She bought his kids ice creams with her first pay packet. Her memories of him were of a huge man, quiet, distant. Although he once wrote her a reference – typing two-fingered on an ancient typewriter – it was Ruth Kirk she knew best and she was surprised to get a job offer from him when he became Labour leader. Wary of sycophants, he was keen to keep someone from those old days close. Hayward became his private secretary, following him till his death. Her book is based on her notes from those years, a collection of fascinating, candid detail: Prince Philip having a tantrum, Kirk rejecting a prepared speech for being no better than a 'decapitated turd'. A plot of sorts comes via its diary structure, an ominous countdown, each day closer and closer to what we know is coming, what Kirk knew was coming. 'I won't make old bones,' he told her once, oddly careless of his health, guzzling Coca-Cola and reluctant to see doctors. Finally, she shows the very real numbness of the event itself:

> About 9 p.m. the phone rang. It was Gray Nelson. He said, 'Margaret, I have some sad news. The Prime Minister has just passed away.'
> I said, 'Thank you, Gray, for letting me know so promptly.'
> He said, 'You realise what I've said?'
> I said, 'Yes, the Prime Minister is dead.'

Kirk's early death meant he has been alternately mythologised and forgotten, always talked of in terms of promise cut short. 'We had so much hope when he came in,' an aunt told me, a statement that made me jealous. I've never felt that way about a politician, even the ones I've liked. Always, they've felt like managers more than leaders, with their talk of aspirations and goals. But it's possible I wouldn't have felt that way about Kirk, either. It's the myth I've been chasing. Had I lived then, it's just as likely I would have been impatient with his social conservatism – he was stubbornly against homosexual law reform – or frustrated by his blind spot for economics.

It's said that Lange baulked at commemorating Kirk's death in the 1980s. By then Kirk was already faintly fogeyish, carrying the taint of import licences and government ownership. His story has been updated since. In John Key we've had another prime minister who overcame hardship; the former National leader was raised in a Christchurch state house. In his case, though, those beginnings were always spoken of in contrast to his later success, as proof of how far he'd come – the state house a springboard for the man we saw: the businessman, the millionaire, the prime minister. The signs of Key's common touch (the dad jokes, necking Steinlager at a barbecue) were the same classless japes you'd expect from a blokey CE or an accountant on holiday. He had transcended the state house, so much so that his government would have no qualms about selling it. Their focus was on business and the economy. As that improved, the rest of us should jump aboard, better ourselves as he had.

It's only with the election of a prime minister born, like me, after Kirk's death, that he has been invoked again. It's reported that Jacinda Ardern has a picture of him meeting her grandmother on her wall, and in the run-up to her prime ministership she spoke approvingly of his empathy, quoting his line that people don't ask for much, just 'someone to love, somewhere to live, somewhere to work and something to hope for'. It's been repeated a lot; Ardern herself gave it a thrashing. 'She quotes Kirk at every public speech I've been to,' wrote journalist Lloyd Burr after a day on the campaign trail. But if you can hear past that, and listen all over again, it remains a remarkable statement, humble in its vision and deeply rooted in Kirk's own past, his need to house his family, his childhood poverty, and the loneliness that shadowed his life – Hayward writes of him believing he was unloved, overlooked by his parents. His vision of government was one that should make sure others didn't experience the same. And now, as full-time jobs are shattered into contracts or – most euphemistically – gigs, and land banking is common practice in the midst of a housing shortage, it feels important to hear a politician acknowledge those basic needs again, albeit with borrowed words.

Even Kirk didn't live up to his own words: that resistance to homosexual law reform hardly fits with 'someone to love'. But myths aren't blueprints or maps. He's been described as one of the biggest 'what if's of our politics, a way of saying he never finished what he'd started, that he would have made this country different. Except that I've always heard it differently, and perhaps Ardern did too, imagining he'd posed us a question, asking us to think about how our politics could be. What if it never forgot the way the poorest of us lived, worked to make sure we all had those basic needs fulfilled, and held our values even as more powerful countries forgot theirs?

For all its faults, Kirk's house didn't do too badly in the Canterbury earthquakes. It was only a few hundred metres away from an area that was red-zoned, where almost a thousand homes were destroyed, but it came through with only a few cracks. Philip Dobb told me he was able to fix them himself. Like everyone down there he was unimpressed with EQC. The local paper came by to write a story on the house's survival, and the *Herald* ran a short piece. There are a few years left in those cinderblocks.

# Missing

I don't remember seeing Mr Brown alive, but I know I saw him dead. Dad had worked at the same school as Mrs Brown and he took me and my brother to see her on the weekend of the tangi. After polite, quiet talk in the lounge, she ushered us into a side room. He was there, in his casket. We stood beside him, and I looked at his hands, which were large, strong-looking still. My only memory of the man.

We went to the tangi too, and for me it was a good day. Crowds came and went from the marae. My brother and I clambered over grassy mounds and played tag with Mr Brown's grandkids, and at one point we wandered around the parked cars before coming across a sleek black wagon with tail fins.

'I'm going to have a car like that when I grow up,' my brother said.

'It's the hearse,' I said, knowing this even though it was the first I had seen. The funeral was a first too, and before that evening in the side room I hadn't seen a dead person either. I was nine, ten maybe, too young to know that all three were a part of life. In the years that followed, I would see my own grandparents in their hospital beds and attend funerals that were much less fun than Mr Brown's.

And then, just the other day, as I was hurrying back from my lunchbreak, I saw Simon. As usual I had dawdled in a bookshop, and to get back in time I took a shortcut through a shopping arcade. Its glass doors slid open and there he was, among the crowd emerging. I looked across the stream of people to him, attempting to catch his eye so I could nod hello, but he looked beyond me. He walked on. It was only later that I remembered he was dead.

A year ago, I opened the paper to see his name. For me he was someone from uni days, a contemporary. For the news he was a 'missing climber', last seen setting out for a peak. His family hadn't heard from him in weeks. He was highly experienced, the news said, and I latched on to that one note of hope. But I still found myself thinking about the cold and loneliness of a South Island mountain. A few days later, I read his name again. His sleeping bag had been found. The story referred to a woman who was his 'ex-partner' and I found myself made uneasy by that 'ex' – it felt like prying to learn those details from this third, dispassionate source. I emailed my friend Sam with the news, writing a short note, then deleting it and writing again. I wasn't sure whether to hope or to call this bad news. 'Jeez, doesn't sound good,' Sam said.

The next story said the search had been called off. A crevasse, was the searchers' guess. Simon had simply disappeared into the mountain. No one would ever see him again. Not me; despite my double-take in the shopping arcade, I don't think there's such a thing as ghosts, even if I do believe in haunting. The man I saw was just a stranger who resembled Simon enough to make me forget for a moment everything I had read.

*

When I think of death, I think of the inevitable, looming kind. In one of his essays, George Orwell quoted the rhyme Solomon Grundy, which tells of a man 'Born on a Monday, christened on Tuesday,' and so on, until he takes ill on Thursday and dies on Friday. It represents the 'churchyard mentality of the peasant', Orwell wrote, and it's a fair summary of my feelings too. Time is slipping away. It's already too late for me to be a world champion at any sport other than lawn bowls and even then I'll need to get on to it soon. My reaction to this is either to panic – my go-to nightmare is the one where teeth slip painlessly, decisively out of my mouth – or to resist and deny, to stall on the milestones of life as if they are rungs on a ladder into the grave. Alisa and I are resolutely unmarried despite over a decade spent together. We have only just bought a house, even though we've had a deposit for a while now.

This reluctant house-buying took us to our lawyer's. He was back at work, post op. Crutches lay nearby, and he propped a slippered foot on an office chair. After a long and amiable chat (it was unclear if he was charging us by the hour), he told us we needed wills. Things get messy, he said. It's all right if everything goes to the other. 'But if you're in the same car . . .'

He left that hanging, no need to say more to remind us that the long highway home – No U-Turns – can become a much quicker trip. All it takes is a drift across a painted line, a doctor's frown, a crevasse. When I drove home that afternoon, my hands were clamped at ten and two. And yet the same car was less troubling than the alternative – for death to leave me alone, to take Alisa only, or my family, my friends.

These were the possibilities I knew, the deaths I thought I knew. Now I had another – Simon, a smiling guy in glasses. I wouldn't have included him in that list of loved ones, because the truth is, I didn't know him very well at all. He was a friend of Sam's, not mine, and during university days I would sometimes come across him on campus. He had a slight but constant smile.

Sam had introduced us at a party at the flat. He told Simon I might not be an engineer like them but I had a keen interest in something called armature winding. It was an in-joke – I had once spotted a book about this lying around the flat, and it was the only part of Sam's studies I bothered to understand. It stuck with Simon as well.

Later that night I saw him talking to a girl who I knew went out with our neighbour. That neighbour was a maniac. I worried he would react badly if he saw Simon talking to his girlfriend. The only reason she was alone at that point was because the neighbour was in our backyard, demonstrating commando moves with a machete.

I needed to tell Simon. Did he know how to disarm a man with a machete? I had a spiel ready and was frothing with worry. But before I could even open my mouth, Simon began chatting happily about armature winding.

From then on we'd talk if we met on campus. So often in these situations my impulse is to duck by, not confident that others will remember me, even though I recognise them. I'm embarrassed, too, about my feeble small talk skills. But with Simon, I had none of these fears. He was always quick to recognise me, to ask how I was. His intensity, his interests, meant his conversation was never inane. He'd look me square in the eye. He didn't hedge. One day, he interrupted himself mid-sentence to comment on something he had seen behind me, without pause or break in eye contact, so that it went something like this: 'He'll be busy with wow that was a big jump. That guy just jumped those steps on his mountain bike.'

We talked about our studies, our hobbies or plans, not the weather or sports I had to pretend I followed. Somehow this happened without us telling lies about the need to catch up more often, without those fumbling attempts to get away which begin almost as soon as you meet. And even though we never had anything more than chance meetings, this routine continued into Wellington where we had both moved for work.

An acquaintance. It doesn't sound like much, I know. I've made his death about me, when it belongs to his family, his friends, his partner, ex or not. But I can't help myself. This was someone who could make me feel a part of something – a city, a community – and now he's gone. Perhaps this was the way my father felt about Mr Brown; how those unfamiliar, elderly faces felt at my grandparents' funerals.

We hurry on from home to work, from friend to family. The reasons to stop and talk decreasing, the world less friendly for some reason, because aren't our dearest still close? And then one day you see a dead man walking. You read a story in the news and find a different sort of missing. It is a missing all the same.

# Hard Sleep

Many, many mornings, I try for a sleep on the train. This I attempt as the track rises towards the darkness of the Remutaka tunnel. I stretch out my legs, arrange my arms loosely in my lap. The seats have slight wings which cup my head just enough that it slightly rocks with the rattle of steel wheels on steel rails. Eyes closed, I listen to the clack of those wheels, the snuffy whistle of others sleeping around me and, more often than not, I remain wide awake. Sometimes though, just sometimes, I emerge from the tunnel asleep, and midway through the Hutt Valley I wake up, feeling close to drowned. This sleep, too brief to provide any refreshment, leaves me half awake and wanting back into snoozeville for the rest of the day. I struggle on, foggy and unable to hold a thought, cowering from small talk, from all talk really. In this way, that brief nap on the train is the best predictor I have of a bad day, and yet I never stop attempting it, craving train sleep, the best I have discovered. Sleep is sleep, you may think, but you'd be wrong. There is something luxurious about giving in to heavy eyes, letting slumber wash over you, all the while carried along, the wheels beneath blurring to clouds, a moving cushion, blissfully zonked and completely in the care of KiwiRail.

This phenomenon I first discovered in China, and have repeated in other countries since, drawn to those two magic words: night train. I can report that of them all, the Spanish were the most luxe, offering a four-bunk cabin and a plastic-wrapped toothbrush, although the cabins were segregated by Señoras and Caballeros, so Alisa and I would have to compare notes on arrival. In America, Amtrak was good if expensive, and they fed us silly. I got hooked on their enormous meals, and on the day we were due to arrive I crept out at dawn, determined not to miss my final, included-in-the-ticket-price, gargantuan breakfast.

'That was one hell of a night, huh?' an elderly Californian said over his waffles.

'Sure was,' I said, tucking in and oblivious, and it was only as we continued to chat that I learnt I'd slept right through not only a midnight breakdown but the train reversing for five hours back to another station, where they then changed engines.

The Russian trains we took were of the Soviet era, filled with young men returning from military service in the east – they wore the most swashbuckling uniform: dark jackets over Breton shirts, and beribboned hats, and these outfits matched the theatrical returns they made to their hometowns, stepping down with arms outstretched, kissing the air, as babushkas and girlfriends swooned. But between stops, they sat quietly. I vividly remember one man eating cucumbers which he dipped into a catering-sized bucket of mayonnaise. We all shared the open space of a third-class carriage, ingeniously filled with bunks and seats that folded into beds. These carriages were clean even if they smelt of feet and the smoked fish that were sold at each stop and, again, I slept well. A few of those men got drunk, and one had to be carried to the toilets, but they did so silently, solemnly really. There was a respect for the shared space, the sanctity of a good night's snooze on the train.

But it was in China that I have spent the most time asleep on wheels. Alisa and I lived there for almost a year in a big city I had never heard of until a few months before our arrival. We were English teachers at a university, living and working in a collection of seamy concrete buildings behind a lily pond. English teaching was a job we'd done before in Japan and this, as well as having a degree earned in an English-speaking country, were all the qualifications we needed. Teaching came with long holidays, and we spent these travelling by train to other provinces, to cities in the north, east, south and west. We went to Hunan, from where Chairman Mao hailed, and to Beijing where he lay, a pale-pink mummy in a glass coffin. We went to Sichuan to eat food that made us sweat, to subtropical Yunnan, and dirt-poor Henan.

China is a communist country but class is everywhere, and its trains offered several types of seat and berth, each a slight graduation from the next in status and comfort. We most commonly travelled in something known as 'hard sleep'. A misnomer, it refers to bunks of three, not hard at all, all facing another set of three. There is a partition between each set of bunks but, as in those Russian trains, it was an open space so you could wander past the sleepers. This equated to second class. First was known as 'soft sleep', the bunks not actually softer but limited to four within an actual room that contained a thermos of hot water and a doily. Still, hard sleep was comfortable enough, capable of inducing that incredible blissful sleep. I lay wrapped in China Railway's clean and starchy sheets. The non-stop of wheels on rails, a universal language, translated through springs and the frame of a bunk bolted to the cabin wall, to a gentle rocking, the sensation of floating, cocooned and carried on through the night, out of it for hours and dreaming pleasant, unmemorable dreams.

Our living in China was itself the extension of a dream. In the years leading up to our trip, I had read stories in the news about China as some sort of frontier, a place where people went into business and found new callings. The country's growing middle class were keen for things we took for granted, whether it was milk or English lessons, and it meant there were opportunities for the mediocre. These stories were like those of someone transported back in time, able to wow people with something commonplace like a wristwatch. I inhaled them. I saw myself as some new version of the old China hand, falling backwards into some job more exciting than teaching. These were the musings of someone who spent too much time gazing at breathless news stories on a screen, yes. But also those of someone drunk on privilege, something helped along by the ease with which I'd got a job there, and bolstered too, I think, by years of reading travel writing. It is a form I love and will always love in some way, but it is also one reliant more often than not on a shaky premise: the notion that being in some remote place, backed maybe with a little research and nosiness, will give a literate Westerner something interesting to say. I devoured books of this kind on China. I read very little written by an actual Chinese person. Absurd, I see now, and absurd too to think that in a country of more than a billion I would have something unique to offer.

Still, it would take arrival for this to be helpfully knocked out of my system. I found no other job. In fact, I was barely needed at the one I did. 'University' didn't have the cachet I expected, and I stood before forty bored twenty-somethings, my lessons in competition with their conversations, phones or need of a nap. There it was clearer why I had so easily won the role: I was a box ticked, a token. They could now say they had a number of native-speaking teachers on staff, and the content of my classes, no matter how hard I tried, was barely of any interest to either my pupils or employers. The minute I turned to the blackboard – the university still ran on chalk – I heard the jangle of video games beginning, a dozen conversations resuming. Oh well, at least I wasn't as bad as the poor drudge who taught Marxism. Occasionally I'd peer through the glass door to see him sitting at his desk with a microphone clamped to his face – a dismal karaoke, not noticing, not caring that almost every student sat slumped, their heads down, sleeping as soundly as I did on the train.

Simply leaving our two-room teacher's apartment and walking in the streets was enough to show me how wrong my daydreams had been. This was not a place where I had anything to offer, aside from that dubious qualification of native English speaking. The streets were wide, held no place for me, nor much appeal. There were shops that sold lengths of plastic pipe and electrical wire, smoky internet cafés, noodle bars that left their doors open to the cold all winter. It felt foreign of course, but without the gloss of exoticism I had imagined. What I saw was a humdrum industrial city, packed with people busy getting on without me. Taking a bus into the centre meant elbowing and pushing – no one formed a queue, and once at the centre I had nowhere to go anyway. There were restaurants and a McDonald's, a museum about the People's Liberation Army where every caption was in Chinese, and street after street of shuttered buildings, offices in which the work that people did would always be a mystery to me. It was as if I had wandered onto a stage set, a row of storefronts I couldn't enter.

*

It was on the train that I found myself somewhere closer to the China I had imagined. The problems of getting to and fro, of ordering food, of pushing to the front had all been removed, and all I had to do was simply sit and wait and sleep. Outside the countryside rolled past. We stopped in towns that made me shudder: ash-grey, dripping cities bristling with smokestacks. And then we moved on. Once, travelling with another English teacher, I made some remark about getting off to buy a snack in one of these places and then lingering just that second too long so that you'd turn to see the train rushing on without you. Neither of us spoke enough Chinese to get ourselves out of that situation. We'd have to get jobs, I joked, settle down for a while till you earned enough and figured out how to leave.

'You'd be stuck in this Podunk place,' he said, and I chuckled at this new word, 'Podunk', without twigging to the irony: he and I were already doing just what I'd described – stuck in some place, trying to earn enough to leave. It was what we'd done before China, too, working away and all the while thinking about somewhere else. But the whistle blew, the train moved on, kept moving, day and night chugging by, too fast for such self-reflection.

This was travelling. I was a traveller. The small protocols of the train – the hot-water heater for instant noodles, the queue for the sink – were easily mastered, restoring my belief in myself as intrepid. Those shared spaces in hard sleep meant meeting people, having the sort of brief and colourful interactions that travellers crave. On one trip, an elderly man insisted on shaking my hands and declaring, in Mandarin, that he and I were friends. He returned again and again to do this, until his wife yelled at him to get back to his seat. On another, a man boarded with a yoke across his shoulders. A plastic container hung from each side. They were similar to the tanks on top of a water cooler, and each was completely filled with eggs. How had he got them in there? I would never know. That night, lying in the bunk opposite mine, he held a phone to his face and whispered loudly in Mandarin: 'I love you. I love you. I love you.' The gentle rattle of the rails worked their magic. I fell asleep to the pleasant chant of this egg man.

Eventually even the longest trip would have to come to an end. The train would arrive at the station, the brakes would give off their burnt smell, and we'd need to pick up our bags and carry them away. In China, this often meant a dark tunnel through the bowels of a huge train station, and as we approached the end of that tunnel we would begin to hear the noise of the city outside. The train had been quiet, people murmuring to each other, and now this was raucous, the yelling of the men who touted for taxis and hotels. They clamoured to get to those weary passengers and, as soon as they saw us, they would swarm. I hated it. Hated the obligatory haggling, the need to start figuring things out, deciding where to go and what to eat, always reaching into my wallet, always feeling lost. My consolation was that in a few days I'd be back to board a train, that I'd hurry to a carriage where I could sleep secure, passing through a world in which people worried and worked and died, and all I needed to do was close my eyes and keep moving, carrying on through and apart from it all, a traveller, a time traveller, becoming for a time a child again, asleep in an adult's world.

# Eeling

The river beside our school was a slow-flowing and muddy branch of the Heathcote. Willows drooped to it, and at night we assembled on its banks to catch eels. Normally my mother forbade me to stay out after dark, but I had a pass for eeling because, I believe, she saw it as wholesome; boys mucking about on a riverbank, their backs turned on TV and computer games. We assembled on warm nights with our lines and spears, and an ice-cream container filled with chicken blood, which we poured into the green water. Soon eels would emerge, their shadowy bodies drifting, holding their place in the current without seeming to move at all.

Where had they come from? It was Aristotle's belief that eels emerged from the mud itself, squirming out of the 'entrails of the earth'. Later, Pliny the Elder stated in his *Natural History* that they were created by rubbing their bodies against rock. In the 1600s Izaak Walton wrote in *The Compleat Angler* that they were generated by dew; another popular English myth had it that they were generated by horsehair. In the 1860s Scottish zoologist David Cairncross insisted that they began life as beetles. Eels kept their mystery for centuries. In the early years of his studies, Freud dissected four hundred male eels looking for their testes. He never found them. We know now that they mate, and that they lay eggs, not live young as Linnaeus once thought. But still they have their secrets. New Zealand's eels breed and spawn somewhere in the South Pacific, the precise location yet to be found. The original sex tourists, they feel the pull of these warmer waters in their thirties, becoming slender, sleek, bullet-shaped in anticipation. Their skin darkens and their eyes enlarge so they might see in the dark waters of the open ocean. It is in autumn that they begin to move downstream in preparation, and when the nights are darkest they head for the sea. There are accounts of rivers alive with eels at these times, of eels slithering over gravel sand bars and into the sea in their haste to mate.

Out there, somewhere in the subtropics, they mate, spawn and die. They leave eggs that hatch into tiny, leaf-shaped larvae, which then travel back to this country, riding ocean currents. Their bodies change, transform, become longer, the length of birthday cake candles, slender and completely transparent – glass eels. Like this, one by one they enter our estuaries, and in that pungent water they darken, their skin greys – pulling a curtain over the black line of bone and digestive tract. Still their migration is incomplete; the final leg is to swim upstream, to make their way into the rivers and streams.

In the Heathcote, one grows large. It feeds, lives for years, emerging from beneath willow roots for the protein of larvae and cockabillies. In time, it begins to pick ducklings from their team. On a warm night, it darts out at a copper cloud, bites down on a morsel of something rich.

My friend hauled up the line and I rushed in with a spearhead screwed to a broom handle, stabbing into its grey skin. The eel curled around my spear, slowly, deliberately, the mucus coat on its body glistening under a street lamp. After dragging it to the bank, we cut off its head. I don't recall us ever eating them.

# Amateurs

I am a tramper, have been for years. Workmates have known me as such, perhaps because I don't share a lot and it is one of the few things I've told them I do. 'You going tramping this weekend?' they say to start a conversation, which I tend to quickly end: the answer is usually no. Because although I am a tramper and have been for years, I don't actually go tramping all that often. Perhaps three, four times a year, and even then only for a weekend. My usual trip isn't much more than a few hours of walking through dank bush, a fitful night's sleep at a hut, and then another few hours out again. This is the way it's always been for me. This isn't a case of a hobby petering out – I have been consistently lax for over a decade. On moving to Greytown several years ago, I went along to a meeting of the local tramping club. There I enjoyed a free gingernut, sat through a couple of slide shows, and was told of the many walks over the next few weeks that I would be welcome to join. Just say the word, write my name on their sign-up sheet, and we'd shoulder our packs and be off. I saw my weekends disappear into the gloom of the bush. Their hearty company would be all

I would know for months to come. And so I made my excuses and left. They send me emails still, following me with their plans and meeting minutes, and I sometimes read these. They occupy the same place as the view of the Tararua Ranges that I enjoy from my desk: easy enough to look straight through, but then when the eye does settle, a pleasant, obligation-free reminder that tramping is always there, something I do, might choose to do, one of these days.

If then the space that tramping holds in my head, in my notions of who I am, is outsized and out of proportion to my actual experience, it may have something to do with the very conscious way I began. I didn't have outdoorsy parents who took their children into the bush. Instead, when we were university students, my two friends Sam and Gareth and I simply decided it was something we would do. We were flatmates as well as friends, and were intense about that friendship. A micronation is how I once described us, a group with its own codes and rituals. But that description implies that we'd arrived at who we wanted to be, that our identity was settled. Really, we were deciding this as a group, agreeing together on the music we liked, the books worth reading and the things worth doing. The latter came most slowly. We weren't interested in sports or fitness but the idea of adventure did appeal. We began to look for things that might take us out of doors and into unfamiliar surroundings. We would go on road trips, we would travel south to join the apple harvest and to Australia to find holiday work and, at some point, someone suggested tramping. I can't remember who, but immediately we all agreed. It felt like something we would do – was strange, in fact, that we didn't do it already. We planned a trip. I bought boots, visiting the outdoor section of Rebel Sports several times to inspect them before finally returning to hand over my cash and finding

Sam trying on a pair himself. 'You two are going tramping *together?*' the saleswoman said, having so far only encountered us as separate exasperating amateurs. The following weekend, he and I and Gareth left for the hills in my Toyota, before slowly driving back down our street, looking for the guidebook we had left on the roof of the car.

That very first tramp had a perfection I've never struck again. It was as if the Department of Conservation had conspired to convert us, assembling valleys of sweet-smelling beech, mountain streams that pooled clear and swimmable within the rocks and, most outlandishly of all, a log cabin sauna. Swedish exchange students had built it among the tussock grass years back, and after our first day of walking we sat beside hot stones and felt our muscles loosen, before we ran outside and into one of those cold streams, plunge-pool style. It was a memory that operated like a screensaver, a thought that returned unprompted when you sat beneath banked fluorescent tubes. Perfect. Except that for whole hours it had been awful. Early on we climbed a steep bank and I felt my pack as someone clinging to my shoulders, their hands pulling me down. My thighs screamed at the strain of uphill walking, and my back was slick with sweat. I hate this, I first thought then, and I would think it again at times when the walk became hard and painful. When I watched one of the others clamber up, seemingly without trouble, I decided I hated him too. I would never go tramping again. What was it but walking with a heavy pack? I should have known better than to set out at all. Sure there were rewards, that sauna, those pools, but they could be had elsewhere, by themselves, without all that sweating and walking. But I did go again, and again, because something happened when I got home. That weird mental alchemy kicked in, the thinking that shrinks unpleasant memories the further you are from them. Each trip would seem easier and more pleasant with every day that passed, so that eventually I was left thinking there were only brief moments of difficulty, flashes of discomfort instead of hours of ache. In winter this transformation was quicker. The short days, the hours inside gave me a craving for daylight; they helped to shift the balance in my memory so that I found myself thinking fondly about a long walk in the bush.

Recently, I've seen that hate in Alisa too. A couple of times, she's agreed to go tramping with me. I know she doesn't enjoy it, asks how far there is to go as soon as we leave, and watches me with both envy and anger if I walk on too far ahead. She does it to keep me company and to try to share an interest she knows I have, and I'm grateful. 'Don't worry,' I always say. 'It gets easier.' A lie, at least for someone who goes as infrequently as I do and so never builds the fitness that might take out some of the pain. The discomfort is always there, and I no longer suppress the memory so much as glorify it, recognise it as part of why I tramp and why I only tramp occasionally. I'm no masochist, but as someone whose life involves commuting by car and train to an air-conditioned office, who has food and warmth and a hot drink within a 20-metre radius at most hours of the day, there is a particular happiness that comes from sometimes reminding myself that these things are pleasures. There could be other ways to make that happen, but this is the one I've found: walking up hills and carrying a heavy load until you see the small miracles of home as if for the first time again.

It's the Tararua Ranges, those mountains I can see from home, that Alisa and I have ventured into together. They're where that club goes without me, where clubs have gone for decades now – the birthplace of tramping as recreation in this country, and the type of wilderness people think of when they think of tramping: dense, dark green bush, lush and dripping. But back when Gareth, Sam and I decided we were trampers, it was Arthur's Pass and its grey peaks that we returned to most often, a collection of giant waves frozen mid-storm. The sort of landscape that never lets you forget your insignificance, tells you you're just a dot in a damp valley, impossible to see from afar. The three of us had readied ourselves by attending a meeting of the university tramping club and sniggering when they told horror stories about poorly equipped beginners. There was a man who'd turned up on the track with an umbrella, and another who took a suitcase. What clowns! I was well prepared, I knew, because I always packed a jersey. I see now that my gear was barely adequate, almost all of it scrounged or borrowed. I had a backpack on loan, a Kmart 'Snuggler' sleeping bag, and a rain jacket, the defining feature of which wasn't water resistance but the fact that it could be stuffed into one of its own tiny pockets. Thus attired I would feel fragile and uneasy at all times in those mountains, and this brought its own kind of exhilaration. Sam and I once spent a weekend rained on and sodden, trudging along the Deception River. We both involuntarily cheered when, after following bend after bend, we saw a tanker truck through the drizzle, proof our ordeal was finally over. On another trip, a friend and I walked through snow while wearing shorts, and left a trail of bloody tracks where the iced-over surface cut my shins.

Eventually, we'd properly test this ragtag approach, or more accurately, it would properly test us. One weekend, a couple of years after that first idyllic tramp, we spent a day walking towards a DOC hut, climbing up through beech forest and then struggling through snow. By late afternoon the hut was still far away and we were still struggling in that snow. We turned back and tried for another hut marked on the map. But when the sun set, we were hours away from that too. We made our way by torchlight. My legs began to quiver. Gareth suggested walking out altogether, trying to get back to our car so we might drive to shelter. But when we came to a flat, sheltered area the size of a golf green, we dropped our bags without conversation. We dug into them for spare clothes and food, scattering socks and cooking things in the mud – tomorrow's problem. I put on all the clothing I had: socks, polypropylene top and long johns, shorts, gloves, a bush shirt, a promotional beanie for a kitchen laminate company and a heavy PVC raincoat that had once belonged to Sam's dad (thankfully, I had taken this instead of that pocket-sized jacket). With my pack empty, I took out its plastic liner and pulled it over my Kmart sleeping bag. Gareth and Sam did the same, although Gareth's liner was a council rubbish bag. We crawled into our sleeping bags and, lying in the mud, we opened up two cans of spaghetti and heated them on my tiny gas stove, before silently eating a bowlful each. I scraped my bowl for any stray strands and then let the bowl fall to the ground beside me, another problem for the morning.

Is the cold a type of pain? Any distinction between the two blurred that night. In the morning I discovered that my boots had frozen – I thawed them on my gas stove – and that my jaw and neck were stiff and aching. It was only as we were walking out that I remembered I had been clenching my teeth against the cold all night, pulling those muscles sore. I believe there were two hours when I actually slept, but most of the night was spent wide awake, shivering and listening to the trees drip and creak, a wild pig's far-off yodel at one point, and, the more constant soundtrack, the lyrics of 'Psycho Killer', which had stuck on repeat in my head.

That night was a culmination of sorts, the place all our previous weekend tramping trips had been leading to, and maybe the closest I've come to death. Two men died recently in the Tararua Ranges merely because they found themselves still out in the open at night, tired and ill-equipped. If our night had been colder, wetter, if I hadn't packed that thick jacket, maybe the fight would have been against the big sleep itself rather than that horrible wakefulness. It was a taste of how badly things could go, and we would look again at our ragged gear. We would think differently about this occasional pastime of ours. It was serious, high stakes. And, if I'm honest, it was gratifying to think that it was something we'd done – that we'd survived a night in the open even if we had no appetite for a repeat. Back home we talked manically, we laughed our heads off, shocked and, again, exhilarated. We wouldn't go tramping again for months, and then when we did we crept back in slowly, carefully.

That night was also the answer to a question I'd asked myself on an earlier trip, the one where I'd cut my shins on ice. Sitting on the verandah of a hut at the end of the day, I had watched the valley disappear into the dark, in awe at how ruthless the place was. What if we were still out there? We had only weak torches to light our way. It was a terrifying thought, and I couldn't look away. I sat there as the last rays of sunlight drained, until I could see only the outline of the hills, one shade of black on another.

The sublime is what you might call this, the notion of nature evoking something like a religious experience. You might also call it nature as one large lump. Ask me what the trees were and I'd shrug; of the birds I could say there were fantails, wood pigeons maybe, but that was the extent of my knowledge. I moved through the bush without the words to separate out any one feature. Unable, and uninterested. Any talk of podocarps sent me daydreaming. All beeches looked the same. Nature, the bush and mountains were just the background, the place for the three of us to enact our friendship. The hours walking, the knowledge that we had whole days in each other's company and that frisson of danger – these things worked like a drug, unspooling our conversations, allowing them to drift on limitless and unmoored from context. A random thought, an old shared memory, some gripe or grudge. There was no reason not to voice it all, no need to wait for permission or for it to be apropos. 'Wild talking' is how one friend of mine, Bill Nelson, described this. But talk is only one thing happening. There's just as much silence; long periods that don't need to be filled. I've never pushed for Alisa to go tramping beyond those few times she's volunteered, because we already have this comfortable quiet, the contentment of a long relationship. But it is something we rarely give space to with friends. The routine is to catch up, to go places, to make plans. Tramping is the exception then. In the bush there's nowhere to go, nothing else to plan except to keep plodding along. Eventually I find myself suggesting tramping to new friends I've made so we might enjoy this too, and it remains something I do with those old friends, with Sam and Gareth and others I've known since university days. We live in different cities, even countries, now and so come together only when we can and, if there's a chance that we're together for more than a couple of days, we go tramping. These reunions account for most of the few tramping trips I make, and as I write we're all planning another one, longer than anything we've done before, coming together from Wellington, Auckland, Greytown, Ōamaru and Vancouver, to assemble down south and walk around the edge of Stewart Island. Months out, we're already emailing our ideas about what to take. I've booked us rooms at the pub to bookend this expedition. Preparation, partly. Mostly this is anticipation, the first steps back into the happiness of an old companionship.

That happiness was there from the start, and there too on that disastrous trip. As we struggled, we still found time to talk, to let our conversation veer from Sam's old car to the question of what age we expected to live to. We were idiots together and this put us in tune. A joke could be a word. When Gareth slipped and fell dramatically into mud and tree roots, he raised his hands. 'Just my pride,' he said in a deep voice, mock stoic, before we could ask if he was hurt. And we laughed even on top of a mountain, huddling beside the chewed-up snow of the track we'd just given up on. It was then that we'd first begun to realise that things were going badly, worse than anything we'd been in before, and we ripped into a bag of potato chips for comfort. I told the others that in future, I'd spend my weekends going to the movies. Forget tramping. 'I'll buy the biggest Coke they sell, and a jumbo popcorn.' We groped at the bag of chips. They were gone in seconds, and we licked salt from numb, red hands. I'd wear white sneakers and an ironed shirt, I said. We looked at our muddy, wet jerseys, and we listed films, big, dumb blockbusters that had nothing to do with the outdoors or the cold.

'*Dodgeball*,' someone said, and we all laughed. It was hilarious, the thought of never doing this again.

# Notes on Macrocarpa

As windbreaks, macrocarpa trees are part of our landscape, the gnarled border to many paddocks. Their outstretched limbs offer shelter to sheep. But the timber of these trees is valuable too. It is even-textured and stable, and strong enough for most jobs. It responds well to a sharp saw or chisel, leaving a firm cut edge. When planed, the grain glows – reveals whorls and ripples like the surface of a golden pool. For these reasons, my grandfather, who once worked as a joiner, was a big believer in macrocarpa. He told me he knew of a man who had used it to build a boat, although it must have been the framing only – macrocarpa doesn't readily bend. He himself used it to make furniture, as well as to turn bowls and tool handles. Often a long silken shaving could be found clinging to the front of his jersey.

When I was young I used some pieces of macrocarpa to make a chest. I planned for it to be a panelled box that I would use to store tools, and that would give me practice in cutting a mortise and tenon, a traditional carpentry joint where one piece of wood slots into another. Because I didn't have enough macrocarpa, I alternated it with radiata pine, which showed itself as an insipid yellow against that golden timber. This wasn't my only mistake – my tenons were crude, they made an awkward fit with the mortise. And so, I went to my grandfather for help. Our usual routine. He wasn't a great teacher. Too reluctant to let me try and fail, he explained each task by doing it himself. But, as with timber, we look to the qualities that serve our purpose, meet a need, so I absorbed his quiet, the way he'd made it through life with gentleness and patience, working methodically without fuss or noise. He lifted a plane from a drawer as if it were a Stradivarius. He stopped each morning for a cup of tea. When we finished that chest, I carved both our initials and the year into the bottom. 'I don't know why you bothered putting that H.D. there,' he said of his initials, pretending I had made it myself, that he had only been there to watch.

Macrocarpa timber is naturally durable. The building code considers it the equivalent of radiata pine that has been chemically treated, and it can survive outside, exposed to the sun and rain for years. Recently I bought over a dozen lengths to build a raised garden bed, and these were sold to me in great buttery slabs, described by Mitre 10 as half sleepers. I trailered them home and laid them out in my garage. Later, I began to use a saw and chisel to cut a half out of each end so they could be joined together there, like clasped hands. A lap joint, this is called. Each of my cuts produced a fine spray of sawdust, and a scent that was at once crisp and mellow, and immediately I realised it was the smell of his workshop. It held that gentle presence, that quiet kindness. Working on, I felt the need to turn to make sure I was alone.

The lap joint isn't particularly difficult, but I tend to start jobs in a hurry to finish them and make basic mistakes in the process. This time, though, I took my work slowly. I measured and measured again, marking out the section of timber I would remove. I adjusted my circular saw to the exact depth I wanted, holding a ruler to the blade, and then used it to cut halfway through my piece of macrocarpa. I made a dozen more of these cuts, reducing the end of the timber to a series of thin fans, like a scalloped potato. That done, I cut them away with a chisel. In this way, I worked on only a couple of pieces at a time each weekend. I made this simple job stretch on. I stood and worked with the scent of that timber for several weeks.

Like most New Zealanders, I have always pronounced macrocarpa with an extra 'a' in place of the 'o'. Elsewhere, it's known as Monterey cypress. For whatever reason we've decided here to call it by one half of its botanical name, *Cupressus macrocarpa*, the half that means 'large fruit', a reference to its tidy seed pods. 'Cupressus' is thought to come from the Greek *kuo*, 'to produce', and *pari*, 'equal', a reference to the symmetry of Mediterranean cypress trees. I've also read that it could come from a Latin word to describe a common use for that timber: a casket, a coffin, a box.

# Sex Elevator

As a boy, I was friends with two brothers, Paul and Cameron, harum-scarum types whose play held the threat of the emergency room. They fell out of trees, flipped themselves onto the springs on the trampoline and, worst of all, played hamster with an old corrugated-iron water tank. One would climb on top, dancing to keep balance, while the other ran inside. I once saw Paul lose his footing and slip beneath, flattened out but miraculously unscathed when the tank rolled over him. The reward for all these risks was the chance to play on their computer, a Commodore 64. The Commodore was a collection of beige parts: a keyboard, joystick, and several plastic-coated lumps. Thick cords snaked from piece to piece and connected to a portable TV. After playing at danger we would retreat to their dim sleepout, switch on the Commodore and wait for the blue glow of the screen. They had dozens of games on floppy disk, each a black square in a white paper sleeve. There was car racing and sports, a game where you delivered newspapers, and *Ghostbusters*, which was made Sisyphean and, in hindsight, a bit like an actual job, by the fact that we never figured out how to get beyond its first, most basic level. All we did was buy the ghostbusting supplies we had budget for and then drive around the streets of New York, stopping every so often to trap a ghost. We played it for hours.

But best by far was *The Pharaoh's Curse*. You moved a pith-helmeted explorer through a subterranean tomb. This contained adventure – you dodged traps and shot mummies – but also the dark secrets of ancient Egypt. An eerie arpeggio prefaced each descent. At any time, you might be grabbed by the winged avenger – Horus, the falcon-like sky god – and carried off to another zone. One day my brother and I played it with both Paul and Cameron, as well as a friend of Cameron's who was older and dismissive of us. We hooted and cheered as Cameron ran from cave to burial chamber, collecting treasure. He jumped onto a rising platform and was riding it to the top of the screen when a mummy fell onto it too. Mummies were doomed to spend eternity walking back and forth, and so it butted into the explorer. But, for some strange reason, this time its touch didn't mean game over. They shared that tiny space, bumping at each other as the platform carried them up.

'Whoa,' said that friend of Cameron's. 'Sex elevator.'

Cameron laughed. The others watched the screen. Only I turned to stare at that boy. His words were a poke to the brain. Calmly, knowingly, he had added sex to this world of death and sand. Someone I knew, who played on the Commodore and sometimes the trampoline, had said that.

The game went on, the explorer dying and dying again. It invoked the warning said to be inscribed at the door to Tutankhamun's tomb: 'Death comes on wings to he who enters the tomb of a pharaoh.' When Lord Carnarvon succumbed to blood poisoning only days after walking beneath this message, all the lights in Cairo went out. In England, his dog howled for its master and then it too dropped dead. I had read several books from our local library on this subject, and once confronted our family doctor with these facts. I felt that only he, a man of science, could help me to understand the truth of the curse.

'Ha!' he said. 'Ancient Egyptian cot death.' He turned back to Mum, and they continued to talk about my asthma.

Tutankhamun's curse was only one of many mysteries to have a hold on me back then. I read about the Sasquatch, ESP and ghosts. When I was recently reacquainted with a childhood friend, he reminded me of all the hours I'd spent drawing the ships we would take to explore the Bermuda Triangle. And I can still recall the impatience that gripped me when I came to the end of a book's description of the Oak Island mystery. A speck in Nova Scotia, this island was thought to be the site of buried pirate treasure. An excavation was planned, the book said. The mystery would soon be solved. It gave a date somewhere beyond even that looming, far-off future of 2000. I waited desperately for the news. I wandered the schoolyard gripped by impatience. Gradually though the feeling began to dull, and eventually I forgot. It was only recently that the words 'Oak Island' jumped back into my head. This time I had the internet at my disposal. I clicked and clicked, and saw that attempts to dig up the treasure had continued, though were foiled each time when the so-called money pit flooded. While some have suggested the Aztecs were responsible, or that the pit holds proof that Francis Bacon wrote Shakespeare's plays, these days I'm more convinced that it's just a plain old sinkhole.

In this way, slow days and Google have been the death of every one of those old obsessions. To remember a childhood mystery is to solve it. Wikipedia has quickly told me that the Bermuda Triangle has seen no more incidents than any comparable body of water, and that Tutankhamun's Curse was a myth. There was no message above the tomb, and while Carnarvon did die of blood poisoning, it was from a shaving nick. Harold Carter, the archaeologist who actually chiselled open the tomb door in 1922, died seventeen years later from Hodgkin's disease.

These dispelled, it is the Commodore itself that held its secrets the longest. An adult life saturated with computers and besieged by commands to update my software or repair my 'Flash plug-in' has made it easy to forget how potent it once seemed. 'Any sufficiently advanced technology is indistinguishable from magic,' declared Arthur C. Clarke, a science-fiction author but also an expert on the paranormal. In 1980 he hosted *Arthur C. Clarke's Mysterious World*, a television show that covered everything from ball lightning to the Loch Ness monster. His claim was true of the Commodore, although its magic was the kind that involves cards or plastic cups, mesmerising if a little creaky. It summoned images, but they appeared to be made of Lego blocks. There was noise and music only within a narrow range of chirps. Games shuddered to a stop until you changed disks, and whole parts of the machine grew alarmingly hot. Perhaps better to compare it to a torch at night: a small weak circle of light, the surrounding darkness that much darker for it. As players we lived in that darkness; we favoured the shadows. Sunlight cast a mean glare on the TV screen, and we shirked Technicolor days for the gloom of the sleepout.

I remember one day that was especially hot and bright, and still we descended into the Pharaoh's tomb. Paul, my brother and I were playing when the sleepout door swung open. Cameron and his friend rushed in. 'Get out,' they said.

Paul fought back, unsuccessfully, and we found ourselves outside, blinking in the daylight. We heard the snick of the lock and so we ran to the window and peered through a gap in the curtains. We saw our game wrenched from the disk drive and instead, on the screen, there was a pink blob. We had heard rumours of this, but had never seen it before: *The X-Rated Game*. Something black – a pair of sunglasses? – was removed from the pink. We squinted. Actually it was a bra! And now on screen appeared a woman's body rendered with the Commodore's 160 by 200 pixels. A nude in Lego. We didn't watch the screen as much as we watched them watch it. One waggled the keyboard, the other gave him directions. They moved that bra away. But before they went further they spotted us. Cameron rushed to the window and tightened the curtain.

Back then sex was vague, a disgusting rumour to be avoided at all costs. Once in Pak'nSave, I noticed a couple pushing a pram and was horrified, suddenly struck that I knew what they had to have done. Much of this knowledge came from Usborne Publishing's *How Your Body Works*, which depicted the act with a pair of wheeled robots. If confronted by any mention of sex, the agreed response was cringing laughter and flight, and yet there were those two, Cameron and his friend, summoning it on the Commodore. They were only a couple of years older than us, but they had an interest. They were on another level, while the rest of us remained in the pit below the pyramid, rushing every which way, knowing that at any point we might be carried elsewhere by the winged avenger.

Desperately I wanted a Commodore of my own. The want was an ache, the sort of longing that doesn't come to me anymore, or if it does gets given different, nobler names, like love or ambition. I didn't know then that the Commodore had already been surpassed by faster, more powerful machines. It was the only computer I knew and I needed one, still to learn that each computer was only a partial step – that it would need to be updated and upgraded after a few years' use. (Recently I bought a new cellphone. Stepping out of the store, I turned it on and read the screen: 'An update is available.') I did know they were expensive though. My mother had told us that, like the GI Joe Command Centre or Tip Top trumpets, a Commodore cost far more than she could afford. (Actually, she told us Trumpets were off limits because we'd choke on the nuts. It was only later that she revealed their price was the real reason.) But while Paul and Cameron were better off, they weren't rich either. Their dad was a postie, their mum a nurse. Surely the Commodore wasn't completely out of our reach.

I have since learnt the Commodore was designed to be cheap, accessible. 'Computers for the masses not the classes,' was the motto of Commodore's founder, Jack Tramiel – it rhymes if you say it with the tough-guy accent of a Bronx businessman. And it was a strategy that paid off. The Commodore 64 remains the best-selling computer of all time. They were mass produced, sold in Kmarts and toy stores. That computer in the sleepout was one of millions; a piece of the base metal debris of a comet, falling to St Martins, Christchurch, to be worshipped as a gem by the locals.

Tramiel was no altruist. 'Business is war' was another favourite expression of his. There's nothing to suggest his strategy was designed to do anything more than grow his company and make a packet. Born in Poland, he'd survived the Warsaw Ghetto, Auschwitz and the bitumen mines of the Ahlem labour camp before immigrating to the States, where he would rise from cab driver to businessman. Nothing would be difficult after the camps, he said. He was tough: a caricature of a capitalist, portly and cigar chomping, an antidote to all those stories about T-shirted tech dudes out to change the world but who have proved to be as self-interested as the next billionaire. Learning of Tramiel, I find my nostalgia stretching beyond the Commodore itself to him and his brand of capitalism. From here, it seems transparent in contrast, even democratic in its outcome – he never claimed to be anything but a businessman. His skill, he said, was purely in recognising what people want.

Eventually, I got what I wanted. My mother had seen how eagerly we ran to the sleepout, how hard it was to take us home when a disk was whirring. I had tried recreating some of the games at home, drawing black blobs on pieces of paper and leaving them on the carpet to simulate the oil slicks that made one of the car-racing games particularly tricky. I'm sure too that Mum thought there were things we would learn from the Commodore, knowledge that would set us up as the first white-collar workers in the family. She scoured the *Buy, Sell and Exchange* and sought advice from Paul and Cameron's parents.

And one day, there it was. Our own collection of beige parts and cords, secondhand maybe, but still ours. I would no longer need to brave the water tank to play on the Commodore. Although, because we only had the one TV, we would need to wait till the news had finished and then retrieve the parts from a box and try to remember what plugged in where. It came with games, but sadly lacked *The Pharaoh's Curse*. Nor were there any X-rated games. We did have *Ghostbusters*; at least we did until the day I mucked around with something called Filing Master and accidentally deleted it. That should have been a tragedy – our best game, gone. But I didn't react. By then I'd made a friend who was introducing me to new machines, not computers, but sleek, black consoles with names that made Commodore sound quaint: the Master System, the Mega Drive, and games where people fought and bled. After all that hope and longing, I was learning just how inferior that old beige thing was, how quickly each technology was replaced by something better and beyond my reach. It was like the discovery I'd made upon joining sports teams, whereby I had signed up for soccer and tennis, enthusiastic and keen to learn these games, certain that each was an essential, so-far missing piece of my life, only to arrive at my first practice session and find that everyone already knew how to play, that they had their own rackets and balls, and that these teams were a matter of honing skills that were mysteriously already possessed. I avoid sports still, and I have Luddite status among my friends now, mostly because it is easier to play that role, to be vaguely hostile about each new must-have gadget or app than risk living those left-behind days all over again.

I once mentioned those new machines and games at Paul and Cameron's, and must have explained where I'd seen them, because I remember Cameron asking me my friend's name. 'I know him,' he said when I told him. 'He's a dick.'

He didn't know him, I knew that. I was old enough by then to see through his tactics at maintaining superiority. It made me grateful for my new friend, a boy less death-defying than those two, and gradually I saw less and less of them. I saw less of the Commodore too. By the time I started high school, dust had gathered on the beige keyboard. High school was enormous, overwhelming with its acres of concrete, uniforms and hulking seventh-formers, but I had the chance to choose some of my own classes. I signed up for woodwork, thinking of the fun I had mucking around in my grandfather's workshop. It was with daydreams of travel that I took French. To balance these, to learn skills that seemed appropriate for a job, I took something called keyboarding. For this I sat three times a week in a fluorescent-lit classroom filled with row after row of computers. Each had its own monitor, and on them we worked in Microsoft Word. The best part was the way it began – the programme opening with a picture of a fountain pen casually strewn across some papers. It was more realistic than any image the Commodore could have produced, and suggested a donnish life of letters. The picture soon disappeared and in its place was the blank space of 'Document 1'. There was a gentle clacking of keys as we filled our documents with the sentences our teacher had set. 'Word processing' is what she called it.

My classmates included some kids who I knew from primary school, but many more who had been to intermediates: the anterooms to teenagehood. These kids had already discarded our childish talk and gags. They talked about clothes and rock music and, most strikingly, boyfriends and girlfriends. Knowingness was in; reeling in horror was out. Some of my old primary schoolmates quickly joined in all of this, casting off their old personas. Others found a neutral territory in sports, which they discussed with a new seriousness. And then there was another group again who spoke of computers. This was not neutral territory; they were nerds. Their interests were derided. Feeling lost, out of place, I gravitated towards them and their innocence. I had little to add to their conversations about Pentiums and *Warcraft*, but still I lingered, having nowhere else to go. In their company I waited for the bell, and for class to be over. One day, one of them, a boy who'd known me at primary school, noticed my quiet. He looked at me, remembering something. 'Don't you have a computer?' he said.

I shook my head.

'I'm sure you did.'

I thought of the Commodore at home, humming, growing hot.

'No,' I said.

# The Clearing

The writer hopes that in the following pages he has recaptured at least some little part of the drama which once made these cases famous throughout the length and breadth of New Zealand.
—D.G. Dyne, *Famous N.Z. Murders*

From a distance a two-man saw looked a cinch. You pulled back and forth, making a roar with each clean cut. But somehow they made hard work of it, struggling on either side of a tōtara log. The saw pinched and buckled, and then popped out of its buckle with a twang.

'Steady,' Hawthorne said. 'Just pull.'

'I am pulling,' said Philpott.

This time the saw ripped through, and on the return it jammed again, stopping Hawthorne with a jerk. 'You don't need to push too,' he said. 'Let me pull on my stroke.'

'Perhaps it's blunt?'

Hawthorne had sharpened it only yesterday. 'I'll take a look,' he said.

'Hell, Ern, I'll get the knack. Then we'll clean up.'

They had a break, sitting in the sawdust, their clearing in the bush beneath the hills. Hawthorne had made the camp. The dirt there was packed firm by his steps – the paths he'd made taking the billy to the treeline before tipping out the tea leaves, returning the tools to the sawpit after sharpening. The tent was a perfect A of mānuka poles tightly wrapped with canvas. Inside, clothes were folded. Cooking things were kept in their corner.

'You've really mastered this place,' Philpott said.

Hawthorne smiled on hearing it.

They weren't the only ones out there in the Hutt Valley back then. It was the last years of the nineteenth century, a time when we looked at those trees and saw fence posts, studs and firewood rather than a walk in the bush. There were other camps, other men carving up those ancient trees. It's because of them we only have pockets of green left, this area now parcelled up with homes and petrol stations and takeaway restaurants. I travel through it myself on my train to work, leaving the house when it's still dark, most people asleep, and then look out and think of them. I know their story only from an old book, *Famous N.Z. Murders* by a man named Dyne, which I had picked up at a fair, amused by the economy of that 'N.Z.' and its lurid cover: a hand emerging from a bale of hay beside a revolver, the scene dotted with blood. The stories in Dyne's book are from the distant past, and I have to say I read it only casually, the way you peruse the paper, happy to skim or skip bits that didn't interest. Unprepared then for how many hours I'd later spend, looking out of train windows, imagining Philpott and Hawthorne out there.

Dyne described Hawthorne as serious, religious. A contrast

to the rough and ready types found in most bush camps. He attended a bible class, and I picture the other men out there watching without interest as he set out for that class, them all a little bored at the very thought of such a pastime. Not knowing that he never arrived. Instead, he lingered on a city street. In a shop, he brushed his fingers along coat sleeves. He inspected an axe, a pan and other items he didn't buy. Finally, before heading back to his camp, he stopped to watch four men unloading boxes and crates. They were stripped to their undershirts, sweating, but working in an easy rhythm. Their conversation was bits of commands and instructions – they didn't need to complete their sentences. Occasionally they did chide each other, but it was gentle stuff. 'You need more muscle. What did you think was in them? Feathers?' Both the mocker and the mocked man laughed.

There were photographs in Dyne's book too, all black-and-white, the grainy images of grim men with grim beards that always accompany stories about our colonial past. Hawthorne didn't get a photo, but I picture him as one of those prematurely aged nineteenth-century men: hollow cheeks, facial hair and a searching look about the eyes. The book did include Philpott's photo though, and he stood out among the others, baby-faced but for a pale moustache. He wore a Salvation Army uniform and held a bugle. His hair was parted down the middle, sitting on his head like a book open on its spine. This would have been a useful photograph to present to the devout Hawthorne, proof that he too was a pious man. In holding it to him, he pursed his lips hard and looked up. He had thoughts of Heaven. Maybe Hawthorne remembered that Philpott was idle most Sundays, but even so he thrilled a little, seeing the attempt at approval. He put the photo down, stepping past any chance of embarrassing Philpott by talking instead about his plans to improve their diet. 'We don't need to eat coarsely like the rest of them,' he said. He would buy spices on his next visit to town.

'Oh don't extend yourself,' Philpott said. 'I have humble tastes.'

'It's no bother. I'd like to do it.'

Maybe it is the train itself, sitting surrounded by people, all of them quiet, talk out of bounds, that prompts me to think that this busy valley might have been a lonely place too. Each of those camps isolated and apart. It would have been important to find companionship in that world, something Dyne recognised. He titled this story 'Hawthorne's Mate' and introduced it with reference again to that hoary concept of mateship. It's not something that gets much of an outing anymore. We've heard enough about it from Barry Crump and the like, and we've seen too the dark side of that world, its misogyny and violence. There are new stories to tell. And so, the old meaning of mateship no longer comes to us as readily. It meant friendship I think, but something more, a loyalty, a bond. Love, even, but that word would surely have been taboo. In Dyne's book there was a picture of the tent that housed those two men and in it the bed they shared. Planks were nailed together to make a box, which they filled with ferns and then covered with a blanket. After sawing timber all day they could only have slept soundly, Philpott sometimes muttering in his sleep. When the nights were crisp their breath made neat clouds. They rolled closer. Hawthorne could feel Philpott there, sense his nearness, even though they didn't touch. He stretched out and eased just an inch closer. If Philpott was awake, he didn't let on, but he settled back, closer too, so they slept spooning, each warmed by the other.

*

As the days went on, they began to find their way of working. The saw still stuck sometimes, but for the most part they cut clean, reducing logs to a few slim boards and a mound of dust. When they had a stack, they sledged them down the hill and negotiated a price with the man from the railway.

Philpott watched, reverential, as Hawthorne added the money to his steel cashbox, weighting the notes down with a broken watch. Hawthorne offered him a receipt. It made it clear that half was his, but Philpott saw no need. 'I trust you, Ern. I just hope you keep the key somewhere safe.'

Hawthorne laughed and reached into his shirt. The key was on a piece of twine that hung from his neck. 'Is this safe enough?'

The railway took as many boards as they could produce, and their sledge wore slick tracks through the grass. With his earnings, Philpott bought a new rifle, a muzzle-loader. Some days he went hunting for pigs. Hawthorne rarely left the camp. He spent his evenings over his pots, enjoying the chance to cook for two, sprinkling his spices over the wild pork. The meal over, he sat beside the fire with the mug of tea Philpott had prepared. That was the order they'd established: he cooked and Philpott made the tea. It was on the bitter side – Philpott was liberal with the tea leaves – but Hawthorne didn't complain.

It was also at this time of day that Philpott told his stories, long yarns with a hint of the theatre. On this night, the story concerned a mining camp and a thief. The thief went from tent to tent, waiting till the occupants were asleep. 'If you near a sleeping man, make sure to match your breath to his,' Philpott said, and demonstrated with a few puffs. 'That way even a light sleeper won't wake. He won't hear you above his own breathing.'

Not only did he know the thief's technique, he knew to expect him coming. 'I lay in bed with a rifle like this one.' He picked up the gun, and held it to his side. 'And when I heard him rummaging among my things, I jumped! I pushed the barrel to his side, and got it all back. Everyone else's belongings too.'

'And you gave them back to them?'

'Of course.'

At the end of each day, the train returns me to the home I share with Alisa. We have lived together for years, loneliness banished. Only rarely do I remember it – teenage days with the blue glow of the TV for company. Even then, loneliness was only a theory, because I had yet to know the opposite. Since then the opposite is almost all I've known. Alisa and I met at university, and I have made my life about her as much as anything. I have moulded it to fit. The conversations I have during the day exist only so I can report back in the evenings and tell her about each small joy and gripe. We live in a small house in a small town. We don't know many people here and haven't tried very hard to change this, because there is no need: we have each other. We bought this house, and chose colours. Buttery white for the bedroom, robin's egg blue for what would become the nursery. She cut in and I painted. In the front yard we planted a magnolia which is slowly rising above the fence, and out back are hebes and ferns. Our work too. It's a whole different place, our few visitors tell us, and it is. We've made our camp, our clearing. We have staked our claim together. This is a luxury that Hawthorne never had. He arrived in that valley alone and had no choice but to seek out company, tramping down to the pub one Saturday by himself. There he found himself blowing froth off his one mug of beer, adding little to the talk. Even those topics he might have expected to be at home in were made foreign by the other men. A story about bush work would start with a belch, and descend into a dig at old tight-arse Menzies from the railway. At one point, Jock Montgomery noticed his quiet. 'You look like a studious fellow,' Jock said.

Hawthorne leaned forward, intrigued, hoping for connection. All he got was a lecture on Montgomery's belief in some sort of Jewish conspiracy, 'the tent articles of which reach as far as these distant islands.'

'I think you mean tentacles,' Hawthorne told him, before making his excuses and going back out into the chill air.

It was a couple of nights later that Philpott had shown up at the edge of the campfire, carrying a bedroll. 'I'm heading for Booth's sheep station,' he said, except that he wasn't.

'Oh hell,' he said after Hawthorne explained. 'I'd get lost in a living room.'

Hawthorne shared his food. He listened as Philpott praised his tidy camp and told him what rough buggers he'd seen on his travels. 'Things are different here all right. I only hope I strike some fellows like you at the station.'

Hawthorne made him an offer. 'I need help milling. It's called a two-man saw for a reason,' he said.

Living without loneliness, it now seems all that much bigger to me − a bogeyman, a fear. When apart for a night, Alisa and I will call each other. During the day I text. Sitting by myself for an hour on the train, I dwell on famous murders. It's easy to believe that Philpott was motivated by greed. He used Hawthorne, maybe even from the very start. But I began to imagine Hawthorne's want of company as its own greed, that he was using Philpott himself. There was a desperation there, mine which became his. After first congratulating himself on finding someone who would be content with days working and nights yarning, Hawthorne began, as the days went on, to fret he'd lose him. He saw how hopeless it was to think he could keep Philpott happy with curried pork when the bush was full of drinking and gambling. He told Philpott to buy them both a bottle of whisky. They could have a bit of a spree, entertain some of the others in the valley.

'I didn't think you liked to drink?'

'We all need to have some fun from time to time.'

Philpott agreed to invite Herbert from the camp over and others he was friendly with, but it was just another night when he came out of the tent, waving the open bottle. He slumped down by the fire and gave Hawthorne a mugful. 'Go on and get shickered,' he said. 'Good stuff.'

It took weeks for them to find Hawthorne's body, and it was in what would be described as an advanced stage of decomposition. Evidence of poison some surmised. Is that why it was Philpott who took charge of the whisky, why he was so particular in pouring Hawthorne's for him? Hawthorne thought it was a nasty drop, bitter like the tea, and yet he persisted, eager to show Philpott that he was a drinker too, until the stars began to whirl and he found himself telling Philpott just how grateful he'd been to have him show up all those weeks ago. 'I've been alone for so long.'

He had said too much. Philpott stood up immediately. He rocked on the balls of his feet and, talking to the flames, he began one of his stories.

He once witnessed a shipwreck, he said.

Hawthorne winced. He'd heard this one, recognised the phrases tacked together yet again to make the story: the tiny craft floundering off the coast, the survivor about to be dashed against the rocks.

'We all looked on in horror from the shore,' Philpott said. 'When it became clear that no one else would help, I pulled off my boots and ran in. I'm a strong swimmer, you see.'

There was a whirlpool, a chasm of waves. He was driven back, but persisted and finally hauled out a cabin boy.

Hawthorne was sure it had been a woman saved in the last telling, but he was careful not to embarrass his friend. Instead, he asked if Philpott could share his talents and teach him to swim. There was a deep spot in the river.

'Oh no,' Philpott said. 'Rivers are different.'

It's unfair, I know, to write about Hawthorne the way I have. To sit within my happy companionship and think of him clinging to the company he had found even as he was confronted by evidence that it was a sham. And yet I do, feeling what I have all the more warmly for it. Maybe the loneliness I describe isn't a fear after all, but love in relief. We read horror and crime when on the beach and on holiday, and I, it seems, knowing happiness, look for loneliness as I train to work, to home, to my own careful camp. I find in Hawthorne the set of terrors that can be the negative to my own life, as he struggled to know what it really was that he had found as the days went on and his fever worsened. His sweat meant they no longer shared the bed, Philpott sleeping on ferns spread on the ground, unable to bear Hawthorne's body beside him. Did Hawthorne see the lingering way that Philpott looked at the key around his neck? When he appealed to Philpott, asking for a doctor, the response was casual. He was told he'd come right. 'Give me that key and I'll go buy things for broth,' Philpott said. 'That'll help.'

Could Hawthorne admit what this could mean? Even if some part of him knew, when he repeated his request for a doctor, did he still feel, somewhere deep within his fever, a flutter of joy at Philpott's solicitous response? Was he able to forget his doubt in the moment Philpott knelt beside him to say, 'It'd be better if you can get down to him. Can you walk?'

'I think I could.'

Philpott reached an arm under his shoulders, he helped him to his feet. Once Hawthorne was up, shivering still, Philpott swooped in with a blanket. He draped it over his shoulders and tucked it beneath his chin so that it stayed. And just before they moved on, he reached for his rifle.

'You're hunting?'

'There's still shot left in it from the other day. I'll fire it in the clearing.'

Hawthorne looked at the rifle. He hesitated, and he shuffled ahead. His feet grazed ferns, sending up insects and attracting a fantail. It followed them both, squeaking like cork on glass, until eventually they came to the clearing, the wide grassy bank of a stream, bordered with toetoe.

A man named Phillips was in the bush that day, and he'd tell of hearing the shots from afar, the gentle pop of a distant gun. Later he saw Philpott, stalking through the bush still carrying the muzzle-loader. Phillips' account was the evidence that helped to hang Philpott. Hawthorne's bible was, too. When they arrested Philpott, it was among his belongings. Hawthorne himself, they found in the bush, beneath a rectangle of fresh earth. He would be reinterred on what is described as 'a lonely mountainside', not all that far from where he was first buried. His headstone makes no reference to the murder.

It was five months later that Philpott stepped up to the

gallows. He had pleaded not guilty, but confessed once the noose was brought near. It's fair I think that I've characterised him as a conman. Before the murder, he'd been arrested several times for theft and forgery. He was never a member of the Salvation Army, despite owning that photograph of himself in uniform, and he'd gone about under different names. Sometimes he was Albert Wells, sometimes Albert Wood or William Henry Smith. For a while, he'd called himself Halcyon Maida Stanhope, a name strange even to Victorian ears.

Otherwise, though, I have taken liberties. I have imagined much of this story, so much that it's easier to list what's true than what's not. There *was* a bush camp, a broken watch, a contract with the railway. There were rumours of poisoning, but little proof. The muzzle-loader existed, but I've put it in the wrong hands. It belonged to Hawthorne, and it was thought that Philpott used a revolver, also Hawthorne's, to kill him. What else? The shared bed of ferns was real, and was why I thought there was a closeness there. It's quite possible that I have it all wrong; there was one witness who described them arguing loudly one day. Even so, it really did end with shots fired while the two were alone. The bullets came to Hawthorne as his back was turned, and so it could still be that, for some brief moment, he stepped forward not knowing, but hoping, that behind him stood a friend.

# Boatermaster

My mother worried about me drowning, and so arranged for me to spend time with a man named Boatermaster. Surely I'm spelling that wrong, but that's how we pronounced it. He was Dutch I believe, and taught children to swim in an indoor pool built for that purpose in his backyard, a steamy, chloriney lodge. There, persistence was his method. He dunked me like a witch, holding my head below, his palm sticking painfully to my wet hair. Submerged so, I twisted beneath his hand, holding my eyes open against the chlorine for a glimpse of his waterproof watch in action. Still he failed: I never became a strong swimmer, and I never learned to fear the water.

I have returned to pools, to beaches, to weightlessness and floating and bareness. The surf is like champagne, an old lady told me once in Australia, and it was true; at least, it was there. Here, ours is a scouring surf, a brine wash. A real baptism.

I live far from it now, landlocked but still surrounded by water. The lake is ruined – cow shit and damming have taken their toll – and so are most of the rivers.

There is one we have yet to kill. It flows clean from a national park, the water numbing cold.

I stay in as long as I can, and in winter I go to a public pool. I run a bath. Alisa and I make plans for our child to be born underwater.

# Temperament

I'm not frightened of physical violence. I don't believe in it, so
what point is there in fear? Whereas emotional violence is not
fear at all. It's something that strikes within you, and you can't
counter it with your own belief.
—Connie Summers

In the years that I knew her, my grandmother was a tiny
woman, hunched short. She wore her grey hair long and
straight, and her clothes were bold: black, gold or purple. We
called her Grandma, never Nana or anything like that. Adults
knew her as Connie. Her parents had named her Constance.
Did they know something, have an inkling? Or perhaps shape
her to fit? The name could have come from a bad novelist,
it fit her character so well. A member of a Christian pacifist
group in her youth, she was the only woman to be arrested and
imprisoned in New Zealand for speaking against World War
Two. In later life she was arrested again, five times in fact, for
protesting the Springbok Tour. Both were causes she believed
in until her death.

When that came, years after she had casually predicted it herself, we farewelled her in the funeral director's chapel. A white, carpeted room, air-conditioned and untainted by any symbol of religion. Death's equivalent of a show home. Although I had mourned my mother's parents in similar places, it seemed odd at first to see her there, lying in her casket in those clothes, wrapped with an Indian shawl, too distinctive for that bland space. But those white walls were, by design I guess, a blank canvas, and during the hours of her funeral the room changed. Her seven children filled it, all dressed boldly too, talking loudly and giving their opinions. They sang a hymn about a dancing Jesus: 'I danced on a Friday when the sky turned black. It's hard to dance with the devil on your back.' My father began his eulogy by observing that Grandma 'was certainly not effusive, joyous, demonstrative, living life to the fullest as the cliché of modern funerals has it'. And Uncle Gwilym, who had flown in from Byron Bay, Australia, finished his speech by calling on 'the divine feminine archetype, the indigenous healers whose feet are firmly planted on the ground'.

It was afterwards, though, at her house, an enormous villa down the road from Sunnyside Hospital, that the noise and bustle of these assembled Summerses made more sense. The house was expansive, high ceilinged. There was room for their loud talk. They chatted in rooms lined with bright flocked paper, beneath an iron chandelier, surrounded by paintings: a McCahon of Nelson hills, a huge, grey, weary face by Tony Fomison and, biggest of all, two metres high, a Philip Trusttum of flowers. It was both bright and dark, and it bulged with slathered-on paint. Against all that colour and visual noise, the family seemed mild, almost. It was the last time I saw them all in the one place, and it was my last look at that world, the world of my grandparents.

*

I visited that house often as a child, usually in the evening, en route to Dad's where my brother and I stayed fortnightly. Granddad would come to the door, a big man in a brown suit, all wild long white hair. He welcomed my brother and me with two squares of Dairy Milk each, and with those melting in our hands we took our seats to listen while he, Dad and Grandma talked. Mostly Granddad talked. I sat throughout quietly, gawping at the paintings, especially one above the open fire, a Rubens print of two men struggling to lift a naked woman onto a horse.

Granddad didn't adjust his conversation for our presence, although once, perhaps seeing that we were bored, he read a poem he'd written that he thought might appeal because it included a polar bear. He read it standing up, his face ruddy. Suddenly, for one line, he hit top volume. I was terrified.

Sometimes they would visit us, roaring up Dad's driveway in their Wolseley, the brake lights patched with red electrical tape where Granddad had backed into trees or fences. When we sat down for lunch he spooned out jam so that he could eat it straight off the plate, forgoing bread.

'Now I have no duty / but to be, / and to breathe deep', he wrote in another poem, and when I last saw him he was doing just that, an oxygen mask at his face as he lay swaddled in the hospital sheets. Although he was dying he still seemed large to me. It made sense that we were all there looking at him. I was told he'd been complaining about the picture on the hospital wall.

I missed his funeral. I was eleven then, and I spent the day at home sick. I know it was loud – my brother told me there were bagpipes – and like in the days I'd known him, he was of course at the centre, always the scene-stealer with his long white hair. Grandma had always been there too, but was somehow beside or behind him. He revved the Wolseley while she fastened her seatbelt.

It was after his death, the house less one occupant, that I began to see that her personality filled those rooms too. We visited in the evening as we always had, and now she did all the talking. As her hearing went she became loud, and she used her words precisely; she enunciated. I would greet her saying 'Hi' like I did for everyone else, and as the word left my mouth it felt too casual, moronic even. Like 'cool' or 'eh', it didn't belong in that dark, old house where she sat and listened to parliament on National Radio and complained about the foolish things the MPs said. Once, she told us she'd heard an interview with a poet who described herself as spiritual but not religious. Grandma showed her disapproval by simply repeating this loudly, arching her brows and allowing a pause. It was woolly thinking, she seemed to be saying. Her own views were hard-edged and definite.

As a student no longer living at home, I began to visit her myself, in my own car. Not often – she was still a forbidding presence in many ways. But from time to time, I'd call and tell her I planned to come around. There was always something very matter-of-fact about this. 'Oh yes, well I'll see you then,' she'd say. Occasionally I'd bring my girlfriend on these visits, and we'd sit in chairs arranged in her bedroom, the only room heated, and shout our conversation. She was really deaf by then. 'I suppose you'll want to look at some paintings,' she said once, correctly guessing what I'd told my girlfriend on the way over, and she showed us around, pointing at each picture with her walking stick. She was fearsome like that, cutting through small talk and niceties. Instead she might gossip, sharing an anecdote about one of my aunts or uncles. She knew what everyone was up to. She knew that between studies I did odd jobs, everything from gardening to painting to dismantling Santa's grotto in a shopping mall, and she once asked me to come over and help with her garden. Not for love – she insisted on paying, and when I did come around, to pull weeds and gather up the cabbage tree fronds, she joined me in the backyard and spoke approvingly about hard work. Her father, she said, had been a labourer in Oxford, the small Canterbury town where she was born a few months after the end of World War One. He was a socialist, a supporter of the Labour party, and would cycle down long shingle roads to attend political meetings in Christchurch. These beliefs had almost cost him his job. Someone told his boss that he was a communist and that the best thing for it was to give him the sack, but the boss didn't care; he worked too hard for them to be bothered by his politics.

Grandma was the one who told you what was important. I would ask her the odd, gentle thing, but for the most part I was still the kid quietly listening, peering at the pictures. Sure that she was simply Grandma, in her own world. Those clothes and opinions, that house. You couldn't not notice any of it, and I mistook my impressions for knowing, so that now when I'm reminded of her, by something in the news or a work of art maybe, I wonder what she would have thought and all I can do is guess. Really I have no idea.

Deciding I had spent too many years not knowing, I headed back to Christchurch to find out more about that pacifism and her politics, but also the person she was. I spoke to my aunt Bronwen and to my aunt Faith, my uncle Llew, and my father as well, asking the questions I'd never thought to ask, and quite a few I'd never have dared to ask when I was standing in Grandma's yard holding a bunch of cabbage tree fronds (good for starting the fire, she'd said). I asked about the person Granddad was too. He was never far from any of these conversations, his big presence easier to summon in many ways.

My aunt Bronwen had the most to say of the four, and we spent several hours talking. She came to the door in a black T-shirt printed with 'Free West Papua'. Like the others she was thin, something I've always attributed to the Summers intensity, their live-wire energy. Without warning she'd shout something outrageous Granddad once said, or mimic an accent. It's an energy I lack, and I sat umming and ahhing my questions, chewing on a cracker. I think all of the seven siblings hold similar political beliefs to their parents – left of centre, and anti-war if not outrightly pacifist – but Bronwen, who once worked for Green co-leader Rod Donald, is arguably the most politically active member of the family now. While we chatted, her husband, veteran activist John Minto, typed away at what looked like Mana Party Policy. Great Granddad was known as the 'little communist', she said, and his politics had their antecedents too. His mother once witnessed a hanging. The spectacle, as a crowd gathered to see someone dangling by their neck, had disgusted her, turned her against violence. It was the beginning of a thread that runs through the family still.

Aunt Faith is the oldest of the seven siblings, and struck me as the more subdued of the four – no shouts, no accents. Her interests were gentler too. An enormous loom was parked in her home, a tidy, new townhouse in a nice subdivision. But as with the others, we spoke in a room that echoed that big old house near Sunnyside, full of paintings and Morris print, dark wood and loads of books. She told me that Grandma, one of ten children, read the paper avidly even in childhood. She joined a socialist movement and became a pacifist in her teens. I assume she had her father's approval for that, but Faith told me that when she joined the Baptist Church and later the Methodists, he was upset. 'He stopped speaking to her,' she said. 'He got cross because she joined the Church.' As well as a socialist, he was an agnostic. And while I'm on labels, she told me he was a vegetarian and a teetotaller too.

*The* historian of World War Two pacifism in this country is David Grant. This world pre-dated my aunts and uncles, so I looked to Grant's book *Out in the Cold* and I called him too. He had interviewed Grandma back when he wrote that. 'She was quite feisty,' he said. 'She was feisty.' She gets a brief mention in *Out in the Cold*, as does a man named Norman Bell, a name I would later see among her papers, at the bottom of a reference letter. Bell described her, then in her early twenties, as a 'girl of principle, a girl who would do what she thought right without being swayed so much as most of us are by what other people think'. He noted her interest in the 'wider questions of the day', and finally, as if only just remembering what a reference letter was for, he wrote, 'I should also say that she would not be frightened by hard work.'

Bell could hardly have included himself in that 'most of us' who are swayed by what other people think. He was the leader of a group called the No More War Movement, and as well as pacifism, he advocated for an end to colonialism in India and Sāmoa, and for racial and economic equality. He was a sort of vegan before it was cool, refusing to eat meat and to wear leather shoes, and was quite probably a genius, holding honours degrees from three universities and speaking six languages, including Māori and Greek.

Bell's No More War Movement was one of many pacifist groups formed between the wars, groups whose goals were global. The loss of thousands of men in French fields and on Turkish cliffs, the many more misshapen or shell-shocked, led these New Zealanders to question war and also to ask themselves what they might do about it. They belie the notion of twentieth-century New Zealand as a country sure of its own insignificance, importing its culture and striving without hope of impact beyond its borders. These groups met in parlours and in church halls, in Christchurch, Dunedin and Wellington, with the aim of nothing less than world peace. There was the New Zealand League of Nations Union, which advocated for that feeble organisation as a means to peace and disarmament, the Peace Pledge Union, the short-lived Fellowship of Reconciliation, and the Christian Pacifist Society, as well as Bell's No More War Movement, whose members pledged to work for 'total disarmament, the removal of all causes of war and the establishment of a new order based on pacifist principles for the common good'.

Grandma joined both the No More War Movement and the Christian Pacifist Society, which was led by the Reverend Ormond Burton and A.C. Barrington, a Wellington accountant. Aged twenty she moved to Wellington to look for office work, and boarded first with Barrington's family and then, after a brief return to Christchurch to organise her mother's funeral, with Burton and his wife. While the other worldly Bell failed to gain much support for his causes, Barrington and Burton were charismatic, energetic leaders. Barrington had toured the North Island to spread his anti-war message, enduring taunts, attacks and even the destruction of his soapbox. He was, according to fellow pacifist John McCreary, 'essentially an aggressive man. He went out looking for argument.' Burton, on the other hand, McCreary considered saintly. He was a hero of World War One, had carried the wounded at Gallipoli, fought in Flanders Fields and was decorated by both the French and the British. Back then he'd bought that line about the war to end all wars, believing he had helped to forever smash Prussian militarism. But the vengeful nature of the Treaty of Versailles and the warmongering that followed contributed to his becoming a staunch and unyielding pacifist.

In Wellington, Grandma joined Burton's group, walking the streets with sandwich boards painted, at his insistence, with scenes of Great War-era carnage. She worked as a ledger-keeper and at the Centennial exhibition. The outbreak of the war ruined another job opportunity, working for a man who imported German-made medical equipment. But it must have galvanised her pacifism. David Grant told me that as the fighting started in earnest, many Christian pacifists opted to soften their protest and retreat to study groups. A personal pacifism. But my grandmother sided with a minority that opposed the war as publicly as they could. They did this even as the government wound the screws tighter and tighter on dissent or opposition to the war. Emergency regulations were passed. Pacifists were banned from holding open air meetings, and anti-war publications were censored. This was a mind-bending level of hypocrisy, even by politicians' standards. Within the government that introduced these laws were men who had been incarcerated for speaking against conscription during World War One. Prime Minister Peter Fraser had done time for this, and so had Minister Bob Semple, the man who would draw the first ball from the ballot when conscription returned in 1940. 'They did not want to be seen to be lenient on any dissenters,' said Grant. 'It was also the toughest country among the allies in dealing with defaulting conscientious objectors, who they put away for the duration of the war in prison camps, whereas in the other allied countries, Britain, Australia, Canada, the United States, that wasn't the case.'

Still, that hard core of Christian pacifists continued their protest. They drew up a roster and one by one, week by week, they spoke at points around Wellington: the Basin Reserve, Cuba Street and Pigeon Park. Crowds gathered to hear them, a few to heckle, and they usually only managed a few words before they were hauled off by the police and charged with either obstructing a constable or holding a prohibited meeting. The former came with three months' imprisonment, the latter twelve. Both Barrington and Burton took their place on this roster. They duly did their time. Burton would write of watching from Mount Crawford Prison garden as a troop ship left Wellington harbour, another batch of young lives steaming towards a foreign war. As a pacifist, a minister and, at that moment most of all, a veteran, Burton held his shovel aloft in salute.

Eight men had been sent to prison by the time my grandmother's name came up on that speaking roster – the only woman. Someone tried to dissuade her, arguing that she wasn't important enough within the movement. But, on Friday 12 May 1941, she made her way to Pigeon Park. Word had got out that a woman would speak, and over a thousand people had gathered. They watched her and a friend drag a butter box out into the middle of them all. The police watched too. One young constable pleaded with her. 'Please, miss,' he said.

'Good on you lady,' yelled a man in the crowd. Another shouted at her to go home.

She stepped up onto the box. She said, 'The Lord Jesus Christ tells us to love one another –'

And that was it, as far as she got when Superintendent Lopdell, head of the Wellington Police, hurried forward and placed her under arrest. She was bailed till her trial the following Monday. It went quickly, predictably. *The Evening Post* reported the judge's words: 'Everyone knows the whole Empire is in probably the most serious position that it has ever been in all its long history, and everyone has to pull together if it is to get through.' She chose to defend herself, pleading not guilty and referring to the bible. Always making a point, she asked why she hadn't been charged with attempting to hold a prohibited meeting like the men before her. 'Because we decided to be as considerate to you as we possibly could,' was Lopdell's response. She was sentenced to the maximum sentence for that considerate charge, three months' hard labour, and taken away in a Black Maria.

She spent that time at the Point Halswell reformatory, on a windy peninsula in the harbour. After each day's work she was shut up from 4pm until 6am the next morning without a toilet. Prisoners were allowed a weekly bath. She wasn't unprepared for all this; prison had been a certainty. 'I took the verdict as I have taken this whole affair – with a sure knowledge of my own rightness – and the fact that it is a maximum didn't worry me very much – I had my case packed ready for the fray.' She wrote this to her brother, in one of twelve letters tucked into envelopes stamped 'On His Majesty's Service' that, on her death, were part of a mass of papers deposited at Canterbury University's Macmillan Brown Library.

My sister Tui told me about these letters, and on an autumn Friday, the campus full of red and gold trees, a few still clinging to green, I spent the day in the Macmillan Brown's neat, bright reading room. Ironically it was the Friday of an Anzac weekend, between terms. Only the odd postgraduate came in to fetch another book for their never-ending literature reviews, and so I sat in silence, listening to my grandmother's twenty-two-year-old self: 'My friends assure me it will go down in history but I'm equally sure most people will just think I was in for striking a policeman while drunk or some such thing.' She wrote about her visitors, politics, and the prison work – gardening, but also chopping wood when the weather was too wet to work in the yard. 'I can't say too much about myself at the end of an axe – I'm much better with a small fork in my hand. However, that doesn't matter.' Although, seven days later she told her brother, 'I'm sorry you can't imagine me wielding an axe because I'm not that bad – you will be surprised at all the things I can do and a lot of those I can't.'

Again and again, she wrote of the cold. Prison uniforms were thin, cotton things. June and July bring Wellington's wet, chilling winds, and the reformatory was on an exposed point, whipped by southerlies. 'The cold is the only thing worrying me at the moment and that has always been so.' Occasionally she wrote about the war. This surprised me. I had a notion that her opposition to the war meant withdrawal from the issue, a position above the worldly concerns of who was fighting who. But it was clear in those letters that she had followed it closely, still the girl who read the paper. She expressed scepticism at Russia's ability to hold off the Nazis after 'too many walkover victories' and the long time it had taken them to defeat Finland. She wrote of her surprise to recall that in 1941, as the war began to ramp up in Europe, Japan and China had already been fighting for years. These thoughts were followed by a comment on the senselessness of conflict – 'I don't understand man's terrific desire to destroy and go on destroying' – just as the comment 'that doesn't matter' followed her discussion of her axe skills, and disclaimers followed each complaint about the cold: 'I suppose that it is just the season of the year.' She downplayed the hardship she had endured for her pacifism, Dad would tell me, and she would later express her embarrassment for ever finding prison hard, aware that others were dying in that war. In one letter she wrote, 'But of course when winter comes spring cannot be far behind and I'm sure we will more than survive.'

Her brother wasn't the only person reading those letters. In one she wrote of the need for discretion; they were surely subject to the censor's gaze. For her uncensored thoughts, I looked to a few scraps of paper on which for ten days she'd kept a diary, something prohibited in prison back then. In it she again described the cold – she 'went to bed frozen' on 3 August – and the work some more. As you might expect from someone doing hard labour in that cold, she's especially attentive to food. On 1 August, prisoners ate fish pie and spinach for their dinner, enjoying a 'reasonable helping' of the pie even if the spinach was 'very tasteless'. On the third it was roast meat, cabbage and potatoes, stew on the fourth, boiled meat and swede on the fifth, and so on. It doesn't sound too bad, although the portions must have been poor; I later came across an interview where she spoke of waking in the night, hungry.

The diary is also where she made notes on her fellow inmates. There was a 'drunk' too weak to lift her end of a bag of potatoes, a prostitute, and 'the other girl I understand removed her unborn child by means of a crochet hook'.

*Out in the Cold* includes a photograph of three young men standing by the high brick walls of Christchurch's Addington Showgrounds. Over the wall, they've hung placards: 'Did the last war end war? Don't be caught again!' Someone's bicycle is parked nearby. Two of these men are sombre, frowning in their dark suits. This is the serious business of peace. But the third, his shirt collar splayed open over his lapels, lets himself smile. Grant didn't give their names, but immediately I recognised that smiling man: Granddad. Like me, like Dad too, he was John Summers. I always thought it belonged to him, that we'd been given his name, but Bronwen told me that his father was also John, even though as a Scot he'd gone by Jock.

That picture was taken on Show Day 1938. He was twenty-two by then and had been knocking about the country, working as a farmhand and a labourer. He washed cars at a Dunedin garage. He spent two terms at Otago University and, at his mother's insistence, he did a stint at an agriculture school in Bulls. Drifting maybe, or searching. With his labourer's wages he bought books about the great art galleries and the old masters, and he studied them in his spare hours. He was corresponding with the poet Ursula Bethell, seeking her advice on what to read and how to pursue a life of letters. He joined the Quaker church and participated in pacifist groups, and it was through them that in that same year, 1938, he met my grandmother.

Later he wrote of her as always giggling at the meetings he went to, and when he joined her and a Quaker friend at a street meeting, he discovered that they were then too high-minded to spruik for their cause. It doesn't sound like the old lady I knew, but his description of himself rang true enough. He wrote of taking it upon himself to preach to the crowd, and he 'spouted of the harmony of the beech tree nearby, of starry splendours above that war and warmongering disrupt'.

When they next met, in Christchurch again, he'd been off labouring again and she had served her prison sentence.

Although eager to see her, he was also daunted by her reputation as the only woman jailed for her beliefs. Within a month of their reacquaintance, it was she who proposed. Twenty days later they married, and the following year my aunt Faith was born, the first of seven children.

My uncle Llew was the third of those children, and is well known in Christchurch now for his sculptures: naked, voluptuous figures, carved from stone or cast with bronze or concrete. There were two, lulling on their brick plinths, in front of my grandparents' house, and another sat outside Faith's home, sticking out like a totem pole in her conservative subdivision. Llew's own home was a fairytale place of turrets and Marseille tiles that climbed a hillside in Mount Pleasant. He and I chatted in one of its many nooks. Like Bronwen he was a storyteller, playing characters at times. When I got home and listened to the recording I'd made, I'd need to turn it up and down to account for his changes in volume and pitch. It was then too that I found he'd sent me something more via the quiet medium of email. Once, he wrote, he'd been told to think about his earliest memories of his parents, as that would be 'the colour' of how he viewed them. Of his father, he recalled a day by a riverbank. Granddad was sitting there on the grass, reading his book while the kids played nearby. He called out to them, 'Look at this.' And they hurried over to see what had got his attention. There on the edge of his book crawled a caterpillar. He watched it with them, delighted. 'This awe of nature was the strongest image I have of my father,' wrote Llew.

His earliest memory of Grandma was having to take her some bad news. His brother had come home from school having shit his pants. Llew went to the backyard, and found her standing at the fence talking to the neighbour, Mrs Stothers. ('What an old-fashioned name,' noted Llew.) He passed on his news. 'Oh no, not again,' said Grandma.

For her, life was work, it was burden.

Her burden was raising their seven children; it was doing the laundry and cooking and cleaning and sewing. All the work that meant Granddad could sit on the bank of a river reading a book. Still, Llew's early memories illustrate how different their personalities could be; why theirs was, could only have ever been, a dramatic marriage. 'Stubborn' is the word that came up in almost every conversation I had about her. She *was* stubborn and she was tough, flinty and austere, checking receipts to make sure she'd been charged properly, and examining Granddad's pockets for spare cash before he left the house. If she didn't, he would spend it.

He was a man overflowing with enthusiasms. 'Passionate about the world,' Bronwen said. 'The sun! And the trees! It was all pretty amazing. He would whoop up to Lake Pearson for the day and smell the wild roses.' He was an arm waver when he got going on art or books, classical mythology, things Scottish, Christian mysticism. One story told of him looking at paintings so closely and for so long, desperate to see what made them great, that he was sick. That would be his education: reading, looking, letters from Ursula Bethell. An autodidact, with an almost aggressive need to share his knowledge. Knowledge that he had gathered according to his own homemade framework. 'He never knew the usual things,' Faith said. The runner John Walker might have broken records and won gold, but she discovered mid-conversation that Granddad had no idea who the man was.

He believed he had an 'intuitive knowledge about what made up a great painting, of what made an artwork', said

Llew. Granddad used this knowledge to review art, and occasionally he gave talks and lectures, speaking with his usual high-voltage enthusiasm, a passion that blurred into fury. A friend of theirs would tell Llew that he found himself almost fearful at one of these lectures, and Llew later learnt that the friend had a violent father and had recognised something, correctly too, in my grandfather's volubility. 'My father didn't do anything without swearing,' Llew told me. 'Jesus bloody Christ! For God's sake! It was just instant fucking rage all the time.' On another occasion, after an argument with Grandma, he punched his hands through every single window in their washhouse, and had to go about afterwards with his hands bandaged up as if in boxing gloves.

This temper isn't something Granddad would have denied. 'Between thought and act falls rage,' he wrote in one poem, and he owned up to it in prose too, in his wandering and discursive memoir, *Dreamscape*. There were two volumes to this – three were planned – and it's in the first that he wrote of his shame when, as a young farmhand, he lashed out and booted a stubborn calf, dislocating its shoulder. In a panic he ran to the farmer and told him that the beast had injured itself in a crush. Thankfully, the farmer quickly popped the joint back into place.

He blamed his father for this temper. The man had horsewhipped him as a child, and once took an axe to a bicycle. My grandfather gave these examples as proof that his own rage was in the blood, an unwelcome inheritance, as opposed to behaviour he might have learnt from his father. Whatever the cause, my grandmother would bear the consequences. He knocked her about, Bronwen said, and, by her account, she responded with stoicism, exposing his weakness, her strength. 'It was almost to me like she revelled in it. She held him in her power because of it.'

'There was a certain point,' Dad said, 'at which it didn't matter how much he ranted and raved, he was just wasting his breath. She'd just decide on something.'

Later in life, talking to the *Listener* about her pacifism, she would give his temper as an explanation for why, despite publicly opposing war, he had agreed to serve overseas as a medical orderly and was shipped out to the Middle East and Italy. It was a role that meant he wouldn't kill. Although it didn't preclude fighting. The only thing Dad remembers hearing about his time overseas was a yarn about how he'd come close to a brawl but had backed off. In hindsight he could have knocked the guy out, he'd said. It was 'some bloody macho sort of story. Nothing to do with pacifism whatsoever, in fact quite the opposite.' Granddad's position, Dad thought, was one Grandma would have thought 'half-pai'. Not true pacifism. 'She would have regarded him as patching guys up to go back to war.' After all, in the reformatory she had opted for the hard work of chopping wood, rather than sew uniforms like other prisoners, adamant that even that was too great a contribution to the war.

After Granddad's return from the war they bought a three-bedroom cottage in a Hororata, a tiny settlement on the edge of the Canterbury plains. It was basic, lacking running water and electricity. 'During Summer,' Granddad wrote, 'field flies surged in so thickly we could take a sheet between the pair of us and, stretching it like a sail, we could usher most of them out the front door.' My father was born while they lived there, and Grandma washed his nappies by filling a kerosene tin in a nearby creek, lugging it back over a stile and boiling the water on a woodfired stove. The plan had been for a Tolstoyan life:

writing and working the land. But the two acres that the house sat on were stony and he would need to work in a local box factory to get by. Still, Granddad did write, contributing pieces on art to a magazine called *Student* as well as book reviews for the *Southland Times*, having made friends with then editor Monte Holcroft while on holiday in Invercargill.

Making connections was a knack of his. There was that correspondence with Ursula Bethell. Artists Colin McCahon and Toss Woollaston were mates from his Dunedin years. And it was his friendship with Charles Brasch, the founder of literary journal *Landfall*, that helped them into the home that my father, my uncle and my aunts would talk about most. Brasch, an heir to the Hallensteins fortune, lent them £2000 to buy a modest house on an acre at the base of the Christchurch Port Hills. They were there when Granddad started working at Whitcombe & Tombs bookshop, running their theology section, a job that has surely gone the way of milk delivery. It was a step up from factory work, but they were still far from flush. With seven kids to feed they grew a large vegetable garden. Everyone remembered weekends working in it. They scavenged coke from a slag heap in a neighbouring paddock, and they roamed the Port Hills for pinecones and mushrooms. Grandma made their clothes, even undies. 'Weird-looking things,' said Llew. Granddad cut their hair. 'Pretty fucking gawky.'

With the experience gained at Whitcombe & Tombs, they went into business themselves and opened John Summers Bookshop in 1958. It was a shaky first year. They came close to folding and the stress gave Granddad a stomach ulcer, but they would both work there right up until the year I was born, 1983. They sold both new and secondhand books, New

Zealand histories long out of print, art books Granddad had imported, and poetry. Somehow, through another connection, Granddad became the supplier of New Zealand poetry to the State University of New York. The shop also specialised in prints, hard-to-come-by stuff like that Rubens in the lounge – it wasn't the place for another copy of *The Laughing Cavalier*. But it was more than just a shop. Even now, people come up to me, prompted by my name, to tell me they remember it well, an oasis in conservative Christchurch, a salon of sorts where artists, writers and academics might congregate. 'People came in there because they could talk with him,' Bronwen said. 'He would fling his arms about and quote bits of poetry, history and Scottish stuff and all the stuff he was passionate about. But also, women came in there, he was a good-looking man and – in front of my mother – they would say, "John, just give me a little kiss."'

He didn't oblige, she said.

Patrons tended to remember my grandmother as a grim figure behind the counter, often grumpy. I can imagine that. But it was her nous that kept the lights on. She managed the finances, resisted her husband's efforts to spend all their profits and, on a Friday afternoon, looked after the shop alone so he could write, giving him the time to produce book after book of poetry, short stories, a novel and those memoirs. The poetry I've read is at times beautiful, playful, obsessed with love and nature. And at times it's overladen, as the memoir was, with allusions to higher things, to the art he adored, and to religion and mythology. Reviewing his work, James K. Baxter would write of his 'private language'. At times it really is another language; some poems are in the Scots dialect Lallans: 'Chiel o ane drucken Gode, / as wis ma ain maist earthy, erdly feyther'.

This, and those flights into high culture, might be why he was a 'neglected poet'. Baxter's words again, and although he wrote them back in the 70s, that status never really changed. Granddad's poems cropped up in one or two anthologies but no more.

It's the shop, with its space for talk of art and literature, that has turned out to be the greater legacy, and it was the way they lived their lives too, unabashed in their politics and their love of art. They lived like negatives of Bill Pearson's picture of New Zealanders in his essay 'Fretful Sleepers', in which we are distrustful of high culture and dismissive of causes. Pearson includes 'anti-conscription' as an example of the sort of thing most Kiwis would scorn. Meanwhile, among his prints in the shop, Granddad held forth. He and Grandma organised poetry readings at their home, and raised money to buy paintings for the Robert McDougall Art Gallery. Bronwen remembered being taken out of school so she could hear the American singer Mahalia Jackson perform gospel. With their earnings they began to buy art for themselves, paintings by artists of their generation like McCahon, Woollaston, Lusk and Angus, as well as works by the next, such as Fomison and Jeffrey Harris. Art had been Granddad's love and it became a love shared. She would often choose and purchase a painting for him for Christmas or his birthday, dealing with the artist directly and, ever canny, bargaining sometimes for a good price. Another shared interest were her clothes. He'd go with her to the shops to buy those outfits of hers, dresses that were bright or dark, often patterned, and often worn only once. She owned a baby seal fur coat at a time when they couldn't afford a washing machine. One ensemble included a one-hundred-year-old Chinese Mandarin's jacket. Bit by bit they were creating that world I would remember, and when most of their kids left home they moved to the house near Sunnyside. They filled it with those paintings – they would own over eighty original works by the time she died. He took out a loan to put in the parquet floor. He hung the flock wallpaper himself – much swearing was involved – and he painted the joinery white, chocolate and gold.

Over these years she continued to keep up with politics, to take stands. Her pacifism hadn't stopped with that prison sentence and she joined an organisation that supported conscientious objectors, again the first woman to be involved. She and Granddad both protested the Vietnam War and the Springbok Tour, and in those causes hers was the larger presence. At Aunt Faith's I was shown a photograph from the Tour days: Grandma being lifted from the ground by two policemen. You can't see her face, but she's easy to spot – the only protester in a fur coat. It was taken on one of the five occasions that she was arrested. Granddad was arrested too, but not quite so often. 'You'd be worried about him getting arrested because he'd lose his cool,' said Bronwen. Grandma's quiet stubbornness was the greater strength. In court, she quoted South African anti-apartheid activist Bram Fischer, and she also said, in her own words, 'Because I believe that not the law but my own conscience is what I must live by I do not see myself as guilty.' She was let off without conviction.

There were smaller causes too. At the movies she never stood for 'God Save the Queen'. It's not surprising that her sons were forbidden from attending Cadets, but Scouts was out too because girls were barred. Bronwen remembers that when her parents learnt a classmate couldn't afford to go on school camp, they contacted the school and offered to pay.

I wondered what the authorities had made of all this. Had spies been keeping tabs? I fired off an email to the SIS. There was a file, the acting director replied, but they'd destroyed it in 1994; presumably an elderly pacifist didn't hold much of a threat by then. She noted that Grandma herself had beat me to it – she'd asked them the same thing only a few weeks before she died.

Since her death, each Anzac Day reminds me of Grandma and those causes. I'd always been fairly ambivalent about the day myself. I understand the need to mourn those killed – my own ancestors included – and yet something about it feels at odds, a betrayal of my family's pacifist streak. This year, I took my usual approach to this moral dilemma. I ignored it altogether, sticking around home to paint the lounge, the radio tuned away from the news to a classic hits station. Even so, the day was unavoidable. Every half hour, between the Drifters and the Beach Boys, the station faded in the 'Last Post' and an announcer said something about remembering the dead at Gallipoli, men who had 'fought for our freedom'. That phrase made me pause, put down my paint roller, struck at this way of describing our part in a British-led attempt at invading Turkey. It sounded so deeply strange to me. It was this, I realised, that kept me away, the feeling that we were being asked to do more than mourn loss, that we were being asked to justify, even celebrate, the actions of our military.

I don't consider myself a pacifist the way my grandmother did. I haven't seen reason for any of the wars that have occurred within my lifetime, but then I would probably defend myself if attacked, nor could I ever rule out the need for force if it meant protecting the innocent (I appreciate that this has rarely been a driver of conflict, despite what's claimed). In interviews, Grandma said she disagreed with force even in those cases; words were all a pacifist had. I don't know then how she responded to the question of the Holocaust. It was never asked. David Grant told me it had been beyond his brief. He believed that in those early years of the war, New Zealand's pacifists wouldn't have known about it. That may be – although I do note that A.C. Barrington had, unsuccessfully, lobbied the government to take in Jewish refugees – but Grandma would have learnt in the years following, and her beliefs didn't change. I can only assume, then, she would have believed in opposing genocide with the same methods.

The feeling that we might disagree or be at odds was likely a factor in my reticence to ask her more about her beliefs. I've inherited just as much from the other side of my family and my other grandparents, the Donagheys, in this sense. They were a couple of working-class Kiwis who worked hard to buy themselves comforts and were always careful not to cause a fuss. Really, though, it doesn't matter whether I agreed or not. Her stance was for free speech as much as anything. She hadn't even mentioned the war when she was made to come down from her soapbox. Merely the possibility that she might have was enough to arrest her. We may think only force would have stopped Hitler, and at the same time recognise the courage that she, Burton, Barrington, Bell and all the others showed, and recognise the need for someone to publicly question the decision to fight and to force others to give their lives. Every cause needs the prodding of a conscience.

Grandma always stayed away from Anzac Day herself, but she once gave an interview expressing her disappointment that pacifists and conscientious objectors were not given greater recognition. The jingoism of Anzac Day persists, but year by year I see parts of that other story beginning to be told. There are signs that our opinions are not so clear-cut. On the same day that I painted and did my best to steer clear, the radio announcer reported that a twelve-year-old boy had berated two peace protesters at the National War Memorial when they laid a wreath for civilians killed by our SAS. He accused them of disrespect, arguing that their protest was inappropriate. To me his response was unsurprising; for many the day has become sacrosanct. What was unexpected, though, were the opinion columns I read in the week that followed, all of which warned against such shutting down of dissent or disagreement. 'Let's keep our dignified remembrance intact and not let it become infected by nationalist virtues,' wrote reporter Tony Wright. 'It is a special day – but war is only a part of our history.'

On Anzac Day the year before, peace protesters in Wellington erected a temporary sculpture of World War One objector Archibald Baxter, depicting him with his hands bound behind him, recalling the so-called field punishment he'd endured for his beliefs. There are calls for something permanent, and Dunedin is already taking that step, planning a monument to Baxter and others.

My grandmother didn't live to see any of this, but some recognition of this past had already surfaced in the last years of her life. 'She was very pleased,' Dad said, to see conscientious objection discussed. She would have been delighted then, although I can't imagine her showing it, to learn that for his first Anzac Day as Prime Minister, Bill English chose to read a passage by her old friend and fellow pacifist Ormond Burton. Once dismissed by a judge as a crank, his words would be heard again. It seems we're very gradually becoming willing to admit to this side of our natures, to acknowledge that for all that talk of Gallipoli as the birthplace of our sense of nationhood, there is, from the Moriori of Rēkohu / the Chatham Islands, to Parihaka, to World War One objectors, a long tradition of pacifism and peace-seeking in this country.

\*

My grandmother was conservative when it came to sexual politics and dismissive of feminism. Typical for her generation, maybe, but she applied this opposition with the same vehemence she brought to those other causes. When Uncle Llew began living with his partner Rose in 1977, Grandma refused to let her or her children into the house because Rose and Llew weren't married. She set this rule and stuck to it until Rose's death. 'I think I would have been treated better if I was a criminal,' Llew told me. 'If I had been in prison or something like that than living my own personal life.' He saw very little of his mother from that point on, and she never saw the home that he and Rose built together. Officially this rule was hers and Granddad's both, but Granddad would sometimes sneak away to visit Llew and Rose. 'It says to me that he had more warmth and more compassion than my mother,' Llew said. Although he acknowledged her pacifism and politics as a major influence on his life – he was beaten in custody during the Springbok Tours – he thought of her with cynicism still.

Over the years I sometimes spoke to others about Grandma, and Granddad too. I was proud of her principles and love of the arts, and there's shock value in having a granny who did time. But I rarely if ever discussed that part – her stance against Llew. It was painful to consider, needlessly cruel, not only to him and Rose, but to Grandma herself. It was, I assumed, based in religion, and that is how she was able to hold it alongside otherwise liberal views. Christian moralism would have been the common ground, from pacifism onward. Ormond Burton believed that a Christian faith was essential to true pacifism; only it could provide the fundament needed to hold such a position strongly.

But as I prepared to write this, I watched a video, an interview Grandma gave for a documentary, where, sitting in a blue blouse beside the fireplace, the Rubens out of shot, she says quite plainly that she was a pacifist first, a Christian later. 'There are some pacifists who are only pacifists because they are Christians,' she said, careful to make that distinction. I learnt too that she was never really a churchgoer. Granddad was the one with the stronger faith. He had attended Anglican services alone, to her suspicion. 'Your mother thinks I go there to see the women's legs,' he'd told Bronwen. 'If she could only see them!'

It wasn't religion, then, but her own dogma and personality. 'Temperament' is the word she would have used. If she had been a man during the war, she once said, she would have begun her protest in the first possible place by refusing to register for service. But if her beliefs had been different, if she had believed in the war, she would have volunteered rather than be conscripted. Complete commitment was the only way to do things, and she was rigid in other areas of life too – a stickler for routine, always needing to know today what tomorrow would bring. She ate plainly. She seldom travelled.

I remember clearly one evening at Grandma and Granddad's. My brother and I had turned up with a helium balloon, an A&P show souvenir, and while the adults talked we batted it about, jerking it on its string. For a second I let go, and instantly the balloon floated up, nudging past the chandelier, coming to rest against the plaster grapes and cherubs that decorated the ceiling – way out of reach. Granddad balanced on top of a chair, knocking against the Trusttum as he unsuccessfully fished for it with a broom. This was more fun than poetry, and I gave him some advice. 'Try squeezing it against the wall,' I said.

'Shut up,' he said.

Grandma laughed, and I went silent, shocked not so much by what he had said but by her reaction. I was used to the shower of praise and soft drink I got from my other grandparents, whom I called Nan and Garg. I wasn't prepared for his flash of temper, however slight, and her endorsement of it. I wanted her to be warmer, more of a nana, to be easy-going even – a descriptor she would have regarded with horror. It's something I stopped thinking as I grew older and I visited her myself, able to relate to her a little more, to find interest in our conversations. And yet I wonder now if she might have wanted it too, if only she'd known how.

In the very last years of her life she was almost entirely holed up in the bedroom of that huge house, using an oak tea-trolley as a walker to make her way down the long hallway to get outside to the toilet at the other end of the porch. Once she asked me about my other grandfather, someone she wouldn't have seen in decades. How was he doing now that he was alone too? She worried that my sister had spent too much on the photographs she'd sent, and she asked me about the others, my brother and the rest of my siblings. She talked about politics too, and the things she'd heard on the radio or seen in the news. She was extremely disappointed by the menswear at the fashion awards. Someone had bought her a new heater and she wondered aloud about the point. 'I won't be here next winter anyway.'

And she talked about Granddad. She'd tell me his opinion at any mention of a book or a painting. Once, she said a cat had turned up, was hanging around. 'I don't want to send it away in case it's Granddad.' She said this with a smile and a 'Ha', mocking herself, her loneliness.

His ashes were in that room in an oak box, waiting for hers. His name was still in the phone book. And every year for Christmas, she carefully chose and wrapped gifts, books usually, which she signed as coming from them both.

She told me that she had once considered writing herself. 'He said if you want to write it will be the end of the marriage.' She said this and she looked at me the way she had at those mentions of her death, expecting shock, I thought. I *was* shocked but I tried hard not to show it, sure she would see that as weakness. Instead I tried to hear it on her terms, staunch and accepting. A reaction I now regret. I could have sympathised, and I could have told her it wasn't too late.

She was depressed her whole life, Bronwen said. She anguished over things. Dad remembered her telling him that she found herself still agonising decades later that she hadn't bought a spade at an auction. She said, 'I don't know why I worry about it. It's not important and it doesn't matter.'

'The older I have got the more difficult I have found life to be,' she said in a radio interview, which I only discovered when I was writing this. Her pacifism and her causes could be something to cling to – a 'bulwark' is the word Dad used. From a distance I can see her vulnerability; it's in her prison letters with her apologies for complaining about what must have been the severe cold, her constant reassurances that what she had done was right. But back when I was there with her, sitting in the same room, I looked and I barely saw at all.

She did make it to the next winter. She made it through several more winters, and it was summer when I last saw her, Christmas Day. The family were there, all gathered in her room. She lay in bed, unable to get up. It was as if she had retreated even further into the house. I took my turn sitting beside her for a little while, and I held her hand. I don't remember what we spoke about – she was too weak by then to say much. But there were gifts like every other Christmas, like in the years Granddad was alive and the years since, books for her children and theirs, each one signed in her neat, round hand: Grandma Granddad. She died six days later.

# Smoke and Glass

Our son was born almost three months ago. He's close by, fighting sleep in his bassinet as I write this. He came into the world, pink and screaming, after hours of labour in a rural hospital. I won't pretend any of the hard work was mine – I flustered around with an oil diffuser and the affirmative phrases we'd been taught in antenatal class – but still, I was exhausted too. The three of us sat together when it was all over, our emotions rolled out thin. As he peered at Alisa and me with minutes-old eyes, the midwife brought us both hot drinks, the first smoko of that longest day, comfort welcome no matter how it came, and it came, of course, in smoked glass.

Those smoke-tinted glass mugs, the handle and cup all one single transparent piece. I describe them only because they aren't always known by name. If they are, though, it tends to be 'Arcoroc mug', for the French company that makes them. Marae mugs is another thing I've heard them called. Officially they are the Fumer Coffee Mug, but it's unlikely anyone says that out loud. My first jobs were at places where the hours were punctuated by the thud of the time clock, and Arcorocs of weak tea and instant coffee drunk in dusty rooms. But even before that I knew them well, spotting them in my school staffroom, in church halls and at home too. We always had one in the cupboard. I've seen them since in club rooms, staff rooms again, and the highway-side tearooms where I've stopped on a long drive home. They are a part of the scenery.

David Mansbridge, a general manager at Southern Hospitality, an Arcoroc distributor, talked to me about their popularity. 'The numbers sold, God, I don't know, it would be thousands, heaps.' Their strength had much to do with this. Drop an Arcoroc and it will just as likely bounce as break. The glass is tempered, heat-treated to resist extreme temperatures. 'I don't know if the colour made a difference,' he said. 'It probably did.' They were also, he told me, as cheap as chips, popular anywhere where budget and strength were a priority: staff cafeterias, and factory canteens back when such a thing existed in this country. This conversation, you'll notice, was in the past tense. Mansbridge was adamant the mugs were behind us now. If I was seeing them still, it was because they'd survived. That tempered glass meant the purchases of earlier decades were with us forever. But when I quizzed him on what they sold now, he checked his records. 'So much for my knowledge,' he said, surprised. 'We sell 30,000 a year.'

Mansbridge's company was just one of several that distribute them here, and he put me onto Andrew Ashwin, general manager for the Oceania region at Arc International, the manufacturer. From an office somewhere in Sydney, Ashwin confirmed they still sold well in New Zealand but curiously there was a clear, tint-free version that was much more popular everywhere else. They sold very few of the smoked glass model in Australia, even as pallet after pallet came here. Why might that be? He didn't know, and went to talk about a casserole dish that only the Japanese and Koreans were keen on. It tended to be a case of people buying what they were used to, he suggested. Those smoked glass mugs became what people reached for when they reached for a cheap, strong cup, and so it remains that way. But for that to be true, it had to have a first wave, some original attraction when it established itself in our preferences.

I thought of 'Ten Guitars', a song that has endured here, become part of the culture, but which elsewhere is only remembered, if thought of at all, as the B-side to Engelbert Humperdinck's career-creating 'Release Me'. It's now acknowledged that the song's message of coming together through music had a resonance for Māori feeling the dislocation of city life during the post-war urban migration. I wondered if there was something similar to be found in the history of the Arcoroc mug, some story about who we are, played out in our choice of crockery, and I hoped that with Ashwin's help I could uncover that moment of arrival. He assured me he'd find out – it predated his time at the company by decades – and he was enthusiastic. It was as if he'd been waiting for the day that someone would call from New Zealand to talk mugs. But weeks went by without response, and when I called him, he told me he was chasing the French for information. I didn't tell him that I had already sent several questions to Arc in France via their website, and had a reply from someone called Marjorie, assuring me that my message had been forwarded to the relevant people. 'They will answer you directly fast,' she wrote. That was months ago. More time passed. When I last spoke to Ashwin, he sounded tired. 'The Fumer mug thing?' he said, and suggested I send him an email. I began to suspect that his heart was no longer in it, that the French had been unreceptive, seeing us for some backwater, a convenient place to dump those mugs unwanted elsewhere. They do not, I note, feature anywhere on the Arcoroc website, which instead displays quirky beer glasses and Scandinavian-inspired espresso cups.

And so, I was left to my own, unqualified surmisings. Maybe that tint gave those otherwise utilitarian mugs the merest nod to style, brought a smoky European sensibility to coffee in the rugby clubrooms. Perhaps it was our bright light, our sun unfiltered by ozone that made us feel the need for something between it and our beverage. Or maybe this backstory was inconsequential, and any significance lay only in how ubiquitous this mug has become, so common that we see through it, smoke in the air, everywhere but nowhere, a holy ghost, dishwasher-proof and microwaveable.

The other day a friend was telling me about his partner's doctoral research, in which she asked people to identify which social class they belonged to. Some refused to answer, he said, surprised at how many were offended by the question. Some denied that such a thing as class existed in this country. That old notion of New Zealand as egalitarian persists – we think it is true because we would like it to be so, even as markers of class surround us. I don't mean just the obvious things, the symbols of each end of the spectrum, the McMansions and the state houses, but all the small ways in which people stake out their position within the middle class, able to choose carefully where they live, what they eat and buy, giving greater and greater priority to complicated notions of taste. The problem of having things becomes one of having the right things. I don't pretend to be immune to this – I am a member of the middle class myself. Since those factory days, I have almost always worked in offices, where the coffee is ground, where sometimes there is an espresso machine even, and the mugs may not always match but are clean, new and ceramic, and seldom tempered glass. It is possible, I have seen, for people to surround themselves with objects that have been chosen carefully, to own no chipped or promotional mugs, nothing secondhand but for that selected as antique or vintage. Still, I believe it is impossible to completely avoid the Arcoroc mug. It is found in too many places, in 'institutional environments', said Ashwin, like schools or hospitals. Places that even the most carefully curated life must touch at some point. You might, for instance, be given an Arcoroc on receipt of some bad news, whether in or beside a hospital bed, and you'd wrap your hands around it, the warmth helpful somehow when you're reeling.

This might seem a depressing thought. After all, why can't we have only beautiful things in our times of need? I should confess too that I had always thought of the Arcoroc as ugly, a dreary thing. And yet, I was happy when Mansbridge and Ashwin told me they are still popular, hard to break and never going away. That old egalitarian New Zealand was a myth. Ask anyone the slightest bit different from most. But it's true, I think, that with fewer choices we once had more in common. There are so many New Zealands now, so many ways to live, options that increase exponentially with money. Couldn't it be a comfort, then, to know that there are some moments that come to us all the same, right down to the mug. Times when we sup, as they say, from the same cup.

# The Commercial Hotel: A Discussion

James Joyce's first novel was set in Roxburgh, Central Otago. A small town on the banks of the Clutha River, home to apple-pickers each autumn and, year round, the owner of the Highland Pharmacy, a man who advertised his store by playing the bagpipes in the entranceway.

My friend Gareth and I were among those apple-pickers. We heard those bagpipes from our room in the Commercial Hotel as we got ready to spend our days with baskets strapped to our chests, climbing up and down ladders to fill them with Braeburns that were a quarter red, and then carefully, very carefully emptying them into a crate that seemed big enough to garage a Volkswagen Beetle. We were paid $30 for each crate we filled, which sounds a pitiful sum now, and did then too.

We were careful because if the fruit was bruised we would be docked. We would also be docked for apples that weren't ripe enough. 'You haven't got enough colour there,' our supervisor said to me, the first time I turned in a crate too green. He spoke genially with a smile and an explanation. The smile became straighter on his second and third visits, and finally he said it curtly, and out came that threat of being docked.

I did master it though, after a brief period of overcompensating, so much so that I got told – the smile reinstated – that I could pick more green. And I came to enjoy the work, to love that place, the smell of apples in the sunbaked air, the far-off rumble of the tractor moving crates and, closer, from the transistor Gareth put between rows, the sound of the classic hits of the 60s and 70s.

It was in my evenings there that I read James Joyce. We were students then and the apple-picking was how we were spending our midterm break. When we returned to our studies in Christchurch I would need to hand in something on one modernist master of the novel. I say something because our lecturer had described the task not as an essay but more of a discussion. This sent the class into a panic. It revealed the odd conservatism of young people, their rigid certainty in the thing they learnt the week before. Everywhere there were questions. What did that mean exactly? How would it be graded? The lecturer looked bemused, baffled at this reaction. 'This shouldn't be as formal as an essay.' I think he thought he had been doing us a favour.

One outraged student told me she had consulted the university's writing assistance people and that they too had never seen anything like it.

Compounding the poor man's woes was the student who continually badgered him about whether this discussion thing was so informal that it could be fitted in around two weeks of apple-picking. I could tell he was exasperated by this line of questioning, but I kept at it, buttonholing him after class, desperate to know and unwilling to alter our plans.

It was up to me, he said. He reiterated the points he had

made in class, and finally, he gave up and tried to change the subject. He told me his son had just started art school. 'I asked him how his first day went. And he said, it was great. There was beer.' He shook his head, smiling with a mix of pride and feigned shock.

This story was a diversion, but it wasn't. He was sharing it as a way of telling me he understood, acknowledging that for the young, university is partly study and texts, and the rest, the bigger part, is the life around that, the beer and the apple carts. I can see this now. I even wonder that he was giving me his blessing. But back then, my only thought was, well that's all very well, but what about the apple-picking?

My copy of *A Portrait of the Artist as a Young Man* was an ex-library hardback with an abstract cover of muddy brown shapes. I had got it and all the other set texts cheap, rummaging in op shops and at book fairs. I congratulated myself on my thrift, until I got to class and our lecturer said things like, 'Let's have a look at that wonderful description on page 34,' and all around me students very quickly flicked to that page in the prescribed copy. Someone read that section aloud and serious discussion began and then ended, and all the while I leafed and leafed through my tatty book, too embarrassed to ask, 'Does anyone know what page that would be in the Heinemann Educational Books 1964 edition?'

This wasn't an issue in our little room in the Commercial Hotel. There it was just me and Joyce's words. Oh, and about half a dozen academic studies that I had photocopied, anxious that I not find myself wanting for the resources of the university library. I read those textbooks and I read and reread *Portrait* until it became both about and a part of those evenings. Thinking of that book now, I think of the chalky cold of an

April evening, the dimming light, the smell of coal smoke in the air. It was Roxburgh and it was Dublin, I was sure.

The days in Otago started cold. Gradually they grew into their dry warmth, reddening us and the apples, before the sun arced low, and the cold was back. It made me nostalgic even as I was there, with its reminder that winter was on its way, that university would eventually finish and I would become a jobseeker, cast out of the structures and networks of study to fend for myself.

Are any of these themes in Joyce's novel? They are now. As a reader I was a magpie not a scholar, and I picked out the bits that came easy and fit my view of the world. This meant leaving the Catholic angst and Stephen Dedalus's changing relationship with Irish nationalism. Instead, I read it as a book about poverty, about retreating into books and ideas on wet days, cups of tea, and serious conversations. A superficial reading, but for all that I missed or ignored, I still responded to its picture of a growing consciousness. Everything that happened to or around Stephen was vital, whether it was an argument about politics or the sight of dung puddles in a cow yard. He would expound aesthetic theories in his dreary school quad as his classmates jeered and farted.

This came to me as a kind of licence to re-see my own surroundings, my prefab and concrete high school, squabbles in the two-bedroom bungalow I shared with my mum and brother. It had all seemed so dull, a time of waiting for things to happen, but maybe these times and places could be important too. They were what I knew, a part of me even. I could think serious things about books and life even if I was cooking my noodles in a shared kitchen. Epiphanies might happen on the banks of the Clutha.

Sunburnt and slightly richer, I drove home with my papers and textbooks. I thought of everything I had read, all those points and arguments made about *Portrait*. There was so much to reconcile. I needed to take that book out of the Commercial Hotel and into the classroom. And so I sat down and wrote about E.M. Forster instead. James Joyce would remain in Roxburgh.

# A Light Left Burning

Technically Eketāhuna lies in Tararua District, but the *Wairarapa Times-Age* still thuds to driveways there, and the town sits at the end of the valley that constitutes that region, at a point where its wide plains begin to narrow, grow rolling. Coming from the south, there is pasture and forest, and then, after a kink in the road, you emerge to behold a concrete kiwi and a dozen or so shops, fewer than half occupied now. The bank went years ago, but recently returned, like a man who'd left his hat at a party, to take its ATM too. Still, there are signs of life, of growth. The pub was renovated a few years back and recently an entirely new business opened. A reflection, the mayor told the paper, of how vibrant the town was. 'Tabu' this business was called, stockist of adult toys. Sex had come to the main street. Death, however, remained discreet. The town's two cemeteries were well away from shops and homes, the oldest not even within the town but on a hillside off the highway, and it was there that a man named Bryan Petersen was buried, aged twenty-one, one of the thirty-seven New Zealanders to be killed in the Vietnam War.

It was while reading about New Zealand's involvement in Vietnam that I first learnt about Petersen's death and I added it to those things I knew about Eketāhuna. It felt odd, shocking even, to hold the two places within the same sentence, to think of that messy war coming to the Wairarapa. This was a view that suited the way I considered the region I had come to call home, a corner of the country remote and self-contained, as if the Remutaka Ranges were a wall. Petersen was the exception that proved the rule, and his story stayed with me, nagged at me even, a tap dripping in another room until, one morning, I drove out to Eketāhuna. I got in touch with Petersen's sister Linda.

At her suggestion, Linda and I met in the Lazy Graze, one of the two cafés in Eketāhuna. There was a third when I'd last visited, but it sat empty now, and the Graze did a fair trade, the espresso machine hissing like a steam train as travellers stopped for coffee before heading elsewhere. Linda was in her sixties, a mother, a grandmother. It was easy to picture her as both, not because of her age or appearance but because of her casual warmth, her unaffected friendliness. 'A bit dickey' is how she once referred to thinking of someone, and I imagined it as the grandkids' lingo, could see her connecting with them as effortlessly as she had with the two young women running the café, chatting away with both when I arrived. She asked about my own Wairarapa life, and I told her that after several years here it had come time for Alisa and me to leave. We had a son now, and to bring him up we needed to be closer, we felt, to our friends and jobs – these were still all in the city. We had been busy working out the logistics, finding a Wellington home we could eventually move to. I had pushed hardest for this, hurried to open homes every weekend, desperate to find something, anxious we might not. As soon as we did, I felt the old unhappiness of getting what I wanted. On a hot night I'd driven our old car along flat, rural roads, the dry grass like spun gold, each tree pooling shade. I felt the joy of a country summer and the intense regret that this moment was endangered.

Of course, I spared Linda most of this, but she sympathised with the short version. Her own family could trace their lineage back to the early days in Eketāhuna. She was Haddon now but that final 'e' in Petersen was a reminder that it was once a Scandinavian town, founded by Swedes and Danes and Norwegians who had been contracted to clear bush and had named their settlement Mellemskov – the heart of the forest. We looked at a photograph from her childhood, one of her family. Six sturdy, smiling people gathered in the garden beside a weatherboard house: Linda, her father Jim, a veteran of World War Two, her mother Vera, her brothers Karl and Gary, and there, to one side, Bryan knelt, his dark, wavy hair tamed into short back and sides by the local barber. He looks like a Kiwi bloke, I said.

I think they all had that haircut back then, Linda said, resisting my lazy characterisation, and spoke instead of a good-hearted boy, honest and sensitive. It was as soon as she began on this subject that her conviviality gave out, her voice wavered. She cried remembering how he fussed over his younger siblings, played cards with her when she was down. On the day Gary started school, eight-year-old Bryan came home complaining he'd had a pain in his chest. What was wrong, their mother asked.

'I was really worried that Gary wouldn't know what to do at school,' he told her.

When his own schooling finished, he worked as a butcher's apprentice, and did a stint at the freezing works too, before leaving Eketāhuna to do his national military service at Burnham Military Camp. From there he went to what was then called Malaya, and finally he was sent to Vietnam.

While overseas he wrote to them. Rereading these letters recently, Linda saw his innocence, their innocence. There was a gee-whiz quality, an astonishment about things foreign, the world beyond Eketāhuna. At the time, a trip to an uncle's place up in Waipukurau was a major undertaking and yet there was Bryan in South East Asia. He phoned them and they crowded around the receiver to hear his voice. Linda was eleven. 'Don't get killed over there,' she told him. Her mother shushed her. That early lesson: there are things we all think that must never be said.

It was 1:30am, Sunday morning when there came the knocking on the door. They opened it to two men, the local policeman and Brian Spring, president of the Eketāhuna RSA. When Linda woke, both men were in the house. Vera was crying in the kitchen, and Gary, Karl and Jim were all awake too. She was sent to school the next day, her parents no doubt hoping that routine would carry her through, help her cope, and the day began as it always did with 'morning talk'. 'Well today, Bryan Petersen was killed,' announced a classmate.

Her father stayed home. He had been told that he had till seven o'clock that Sunday morning to let the army know whether he wanted his son's body brought back, and so followed that policeman down to the station to make this call, to tell them he wanted his son in Eketāhuna.

'And they said, "Oh, well how much money have you got?"' Linda said. There was a price for repatriation: $400, quite the sum in 1968. Her father wasn't sure how he would pay it – his wages were modest. But word spread, and just as the people of Eketāhuna had once gathered for a dance to see Bryan off, so they came together again, chipping in what they could so that Bryan could come home, his body flown back on a French airliner.

Linda spread out a receipt between our coffee cups. Thick, creamy paper printed 'Ministry of Defence'. It showed that her father had been refunded some of the money in October that year – the cost of air freight had come in under $400 in the end. But, before that, the army had insisted on talking to the Petersens' bank manager, first by phone and then in person, to make sure they were good for the cash. 'They'd already paid with their lives!' Linda said. She had wanted to talk to me to highlight this – it was a sore point still. In 1988, her parents spoke to the *Wairarapa Times-Age*. In 2015, she gave an interview to Newshub about it. But back then, when it happened, they had trusted in the official channels. They asked to talk to their MP, Keith Holyoake, who was prime minister too and owned a farm not far away, near Dannevirke. He refused to meet them. It would have been favouritism, was the explanation given by his aides, presumably because he wouldn't be meeting the families of anyone else killed either.

Despite all those calls to the bank manager, the army had obviously doubted that the Petersens would pay for the repatriation of their son's body. I would later meet a man named Michael Shale who had been stationed in Malaya at the time, a veteran of Vietnam himself, and had been one of several to rehearse Petersen's funeral. They readied for a rifle salute and prepared to bury him over there, in 'some corner of a foreign field' as Rupert Brooke wrote. Brooke's 1915 poem 'The Soldier' would glorify this, make a case for a body remaining of its own country even as it lay elsewhere. But it was a notion Jim Petersen had no truck with. 'A grave in Malaysia was no grave at all,' he told the paper. Eventually the government came to agree. In 2018, those soldiers who had been buried in Malaysia were dug up and sent home to be buried again, at the government's expense, this time at home.

Bodies had been a kind of currency in Vietnam. There was no front line. It was a war of attrition, the object being to grind down the opposing side, inflict the most damage, and the Americans used the bodies of enemy soldiers as a record of progress. They collected numbers of the dead to be fed into Pentagon computers. Some collected more: body parts, ears particularly, were a grim souvenir for some soldiers. Shale would tell me that, for a time, among his photographs were some of men killed by his company, but he had thrown those pictures out. 'I didn't want that sort of thing,' he said, and was uncertain whether he had ever killed anyone over there himself, preferred to think he hadn't. In the years since, he had run pubs all over the Wairarapa: Greytown's Top Pub, Carterton's Marquis of Normandy and, most recently, the Eketahuna Tavern which he'd sold the day before I met him at his home in Masterton. The brick townhouse was more or less conventional from the gate, but inside was painted a lush red, with furniture from Bali and two curious paintings: nude men in neon hues.

Shale's connection to Eketāhuna went beyond the pub. He had grown up there, only a few doors down from the Petersens until, aged twelve, he and his mother moved south to Masterton. A reunion would occur at Burnham Military Camp. 'Shale!' Bryan Petersen yelled across the quad. Petersen was popular, Shale told me. 'A hail fellow well met,' he said, before telling me about those funeral plans and his own experience of war. It was a subject I thought I knew well, because it was inescapable. Hadn't I seen all those movies? Read all those books? But there was something else to know, a closeness that came from hearing a man in Masterton with an accent that was mine too as he recalled someone being shot beside him one day, this conversation interrupted only by the slap of the cat flap in the ranchslider and a man named Tim who came by to mow the lawns. We were talking, I understood, about life and death in New Zealand, only this time it was in Vietnam.

'In that rich earth, a richer dust concealed.' This line is Brooke's too, from that same poem, written shortly before his own death from blood poisoning while he was on his way to fight at Gallipoli. I first encountered his poem at high school where it was used only as a contrast to the work of writers like Wilfred Owen and Siegfried Sassoon, who had experienced and documented the mean reality of war. Their work, with its grim truths, showed Brooke's for simple jingoism, misguided and sentimental. This was the accepted view, but there is truth in Brooke's lines. We believe in the significance of bodies, even when they are ash or dust. We visit graves, or at least mean to visit. These places remain the person in some way. Where they lie is important to us, is worth expense, even risk. In Vietnam, Shale had the job of readying his comrades' bodies for airlift out of combat zones, a job that had to be done quickly, methodically; the pilots wouldn't linger longer than ten seconds for fear of being shot out of the sky. 'It was a terrible war, wasn't it?' he said. 'We shouldn't have been there. Not at all.'

What *were* they doing there? It was an adventure, Linda reckoned. All those young men, raised on stories about World

War Two, as Bryan had been. It was everywhere back then, at the movies, on TV, and, most crucially, in their dads' talk at the dinner table. This was their chance to do what their fathers had. She was explaining the choice they'd made. Unlike America or Australia, we didn't conscript men for this war. They were, in theory, volunteers, and I add that qualifier because Shale had added one too: 'So-called volunteers,' he said. He had joined the army in want of a fresh start after failing an engineering degree at Victoria University. We had troops in Malaya then, and he counted on 'a three-year holiday in the tropics, an adventure with coconuts and sunny beaches'. The holiday would last all of six months before the government announced it was sending infantry to Vietnam. Their colonel gathered them together, gave them a 'hell of a spiel'. Telling them, 'You'll be serving your country in Vietnam.' The colonel referred to the 'domino theory'. 'You heard of that?' Shale said. 'Communists coming down . . . We'll be stopping the communists from invading New Zealand.' It went on and on and on. At the end of it all, they were told that anyone not prepared to go was to step forward. Shale didn't recall that anyone stepped forward. He didn't recall that anyone felt they had the choice.

That theory was the official reason they were there; the notion of a relentless communism that, unstopped, would move down through Asia until it arrived at our door. But in offices and meeting rooms, our politicians talked less of this than of the need to stay onside with America, our most powerful ally, and to keep up with Australia. There was opposition within these circles too. In his history of New Zealand and the Vietnam War, Roberto Rabel notes that the Department of External Affairs very correctly predicted the way the war would go. They saw the quagmire it would become, anticipated the way American involvement would snowball, the war taking more and more men. The secretary of defence, Jack Hunn, also argued for New Zealand to stay clear. But when he produced a memo of all the reasons not to fight, his minister flushed it down the toilet. Pressure came from overseas, from the Americans, who sent dignitary after dignitary to cajole and persuade, until eventually the president himself, Lyndon Johnson, arrived one rainy morning in Wellington to bully Keith Holyoake over potatoes at Government House.

The decisions made by those men in Wellington and Washington came to touch even the Wairarapa, resulted in one man returning to Eketāhuna as airfreight. This was the incongruity that grabbed me from the start, but I was wrong to think it unusual. I would come to learn there were many in the region for whom Vietnam had a meaning that was personal, distinct to them. There was Shale for one, and when I met him, he told me there had been thirty or so veterans he knew. Reading Roberto Rabel's book, I came across mention of a man named Paul Melser, a name I recognised from the bottom of my teapot – he sells pottery from a kiln near Masterton – but who, as a student, had helped to found the Committee on Vietnam, one of the main voices of opposition to New Zealand's involvement in that war.

I turned up at that kiln one afternoon and found Melser in clothes specked with clay, drinking tea from a cup he'd made. He was modest about his part in the movement, talking as if it was simply something you did, routine almost. 'Just a normal pacifist impulse,' he said. And he only reluctantly conceded that he went further than most in acting on this impulse: in 1966, he chained himself to one of the pillars holding up the parliament buildings as a statement against the visit of American vice president Hubert Humphrey. 'We just sort of . . . decided to do that.' He bought a suit for the occasion, the first he had owned, careful to avoid the perception that protesters were scruffy students or, worse, hippies, and in the photograph I saw he cut a relaxed figure, leaning back to the pillar with a fag in hand, his tweeds accessorised by the chain around his waist. He lasted for several hours before the police came with boltcutters. 'It was a pretty cheap, crappy chain so easy to cut, and we were carted off to the Taranaki Street Police station for half a day or so.'

It wasn't long after fastening himself to parliament that Melser moved to the Wairarapa. Here he busied himself establishing his pottery business, and protest took a back seat. People in the country were less interested and, if they were, had little sympathy with those opposed to that war. Life went on beneath the hills; he kept his hands in the clay.

After we chatted awhile, Melser walked with me back to my car. It was then I told him, as I had told Linda, about my plans to leave the Wairarapa. 'We'll be sorry to see you go,' Melser said. We had met that day but even so I looked at my shoes sadly. This regret of mine had become fuel to my following of Petersen's story. I needed to tell it. It was part of this place I had come to call home. And there was another ritual too, by which I planned to mark my connection. A few weeks later, I dug a hole in a corner of the garden and placed my son's placenta there – the hospital had provided it wrapped within a flax parcel for this purpose. This practice is of te ao Māori, but I have to confess that my enactment was less tikanga than the satisfying of my own need for us and our son to remain in some way, an antidote to the sadness of knowing he would never remember the place where he had been born, raised for a time; the place that had made us so happy. I planted a large tree fern on the spot. As with burial, we needed a marker. It had been Jim Petersen's worry that had his son been left in Malaysia, his grave would be lost, become anonymous.

For all that drama of what to do with Bryan Petersen's body, his death itself was sudden, without firefight or battle. The men of Whisky Company were searching a streambed, looking for the enemy, when there was a shot. Petersen dropped to the ground. His comrades fired back in the direction it had come. Later they'd find a blood trail. It's possible there were two deaths that day, but without a second body this could never be said.

That was the official version, but Linda had heard another. At a veteran's event one year, a man grabbed her by the arm. 'There's something I need to tell you,' he said. Petersen had been killed by one of his fellow soldiers, an incidence of 'friendly fire', he claimed. And for a long time, she worried about this, worried what it was she should do with this information. Other vets told her the man was wrong, confused. That official story remained the truth, and eventually she stopped worrying, came to see that the ending was the same. Loss was loss, and she was, sadly, an expert. Bryan dead at twenty-one. Her brothers Karl – a Navy veteran – and Gary were both gone too, taken young by cancer; her parents were dead, and she was, as of only three years ago, a widow too. 'You've been through a lot,' I said. 'I don't think I need to do anymore,' she said and laughed. I peered into my notebook, not knowing what more to say, to ask.

It was after we talked that I went, as I had planned, to the cemetery where Petersen was buried, and there it was confirmed that the word Vietnam didn't stand out in that country graveyard as I had once expected it to. His headstone was within the RSA section, among many neat bronze plaques that made reference to far-off places: Korea, France, South Africa. Eketāhuna had long sent its people to foreign wars. I found too that Linda had been there before me. On Bryan's grave, on Karl's, and on Jim and Vera's shared plot were plastic flowers. They were yellow and blue and orange, and brighter than nature on that grey day; would stay that way, a light left burning. The Petersens had left Eketāhuna not long after Bryan's death. Linda hadn't lived there for fifty years. She came back a few times each year, she told me, speaking of the place with real affection. It was the last place the family had been complete. It was surviving, she said. They had a much better rugby team than Pahīatua. She lived in Palmerston North now, she said, and she told me this: that she had found herself thinking life had changed so much that Bryan might no longer have a place. Where, she wondered, would he fit now? It seemed the saddest, the truest thing about loss I'd heard, and, no longer knowing why I was there, I wandered into the old part of that same cemetery, where the settlers lay, and I peered at the worn inscriptions on tall, old headstones. I read Scandinavian surnames and years of birth and death. There were no flowers on these, none for Jessie Lemberg, or for a Mr Job Bassett who died in ripe old age in the 1920s. 'There is a line,' his headstone read, 'death cannot sever.' A statement, a hope.

# At the Dump

This is where the world gets thrown away on Wednesdays, Saturdays and Sundays. The dump out on the edge of town, hemmed in by poplars and reached by a long dirt road, the whole place dusty and pleasantly green. Wholesome even. A man named Craig threw lengths of old timber out of a trailer, careful to place his jandaled feet between the rusty nails. 'It is nice to have a clear-out from time to time,' he said. 'Very satisfying.' This was Wednesday, the day when the place only opens for a couple of hours, and there was a steady stream of people there to make the most of it. Adrian hauled a web of garden rubbish out of his car, stepping around old cans in suede boots. Perry, a retired civil servant, was there on his annual trip, this time to dispose of 'electrics, light fittings, old computer stuff, etcetera, etcetera'. There was a lot of etcetera. He left a pink plastic suitcase at the edge of the heap – this wasn't one of those tips where things are thrown into a pit. Already there was a rolled-up carpet, two large tins that once held mango slices, and wood of every dimension, some of it green from chemical treatment. From this base rose a massif of indistinct, grey and bulging shapes in which only the odd identifiable object floated – a sofa jutting from the top, as if carried aloft by this wave of stinking rubbish, this 'general refuse'. There were other piles. One of batteries, and one of paint tins, and another of metal and appliances – 'e-waste' in the trade. Within this there were heaped TVs, coils of wire, bicycles and heaters, barbecues and outdoor furniture. Half a dozen computer keyboards were roughly stacked on concrete. While that general refuse was, for the most part, an unidentifiable mass, these were almost entirely recognisable, seemingly useful objects all thrown into a heap as if society had gone kaput, broken down so far that such things no longer had meaning. Which is true, even if the end of the world – rushing our way, maybe – has yet to get here: these objects *had* lost their meaning. The barbecues were rusted out, the CRT TVs unwatchable now. We had moved on from them, and here, on this dusty concrete pad, had assembled this minor apocalypse of our past.

Thomas, a genial guy in a baseball cap and tattoos ('Live life then die!' read one), sat in the kiosk where people paid to leave their rubbish, sometimes putting up with their trash talk too. Just the other day, a woman slowed her car to abuse him after being told she had to pay, even if she had packed everything into council bags. Thomas looked at his co-worker, shrugged, laughed. This was laid-back Martinborough. Mostly he got smiles, his jokes got more than the odd laugh. It was a hot day, stinking hot and, of course, just stinking, although no one commented on the smell: a sort of outrageous funk, loamy and high, exotic. I sweated in the hi-vis overcoat I'd been loaned by dump management. Thomas at least had a fan in his Portacom, as well as a can of air freshener and a Tuscany-brand minifridge to store his soft drink. Just as he had remained cheery when shouted at, so he was cheery in the heat. No wonder people missed him when he'd left for a stint in Pahīatua. I know I had, as a user of this very dump, although I was hardly a regular. There were people who came in every time he opened. What did they scour up to dump that often? Just general rubbish, Thomas said. 'It's not just old people but middle-aged people too, and they've got nothing to do and they'll think, I'll just go down to the tip.' I made a sound in response to this, a sort of 'wow' at the idea that people might come for fun. A dishonest sound really. I had always liked visiting the dump.

'And they went to the rubbish dump to look for treasure.' In Janet Frame's *Owls Do Cry*, the four Withers children return again and again to the dump, a place made to shimmer in Frame's dreamy prose. Shell-like, ringed by toetoe, but also grey and full of the smoke of the councilmen's fires, this dump was so irresistible that it attracted a tragedy. The children found things in the filth: a book of fairytales, a set of handsomely bound old ledgers. Treasure. I first read *Owls Do Cry* as a teenager, a time when my mother, my brother and I found reason to go to the dump fairly often. The closest to us was out in an industrial pocket of Christchurch, and tucked within the factories and roads around it, like a secret garden. I looked forward to these visits, suggested them sometimes. Like the Withers children, the chief appeal was treasure, but this wasn't a dump where you could rummage as they had. Instead, any discoveries had to be paid for at the dump shop, a space in a corrugated-iron shed where unwanted furniture, appliances and knick-knacks were dropped off to be sold dirt cheap. I have always been, even in adolescence, too tight-fisted to enjoy shopping, but at the dump shop I had the satisfaction of being a consumer, buying frivolously while still only ever handing over small change.

Over the years, I bought a barbecue and a Bakelite clock, a golf bag and clubs, a book of short stories, and the record cabinet in which I still store my music. I don't think this particular shop exists anymore. Christchurch has since centralised this service, so all resaleable junk goes offsite to a single dedicated dump shop, originally known as the SuperShed but later renamed, virtuously, as the EcoShop. In theory, then, I could have my fix of cheap goods without having to visit the dump, but I can't say it has the same appeal. The dump itself was always a necessary part of each trip, and after looking in the shop, we would back our Datsun up to a long concrete pit, a canal of trash where a man drove back and forth with a front-end loader, shifting and squeezing Christchurch's rubbish into piles. TVs tumbled over, the screens cracking, and then, as if in slow motion, the glass would fall out to reveal the circuitry inside. An old desk would snap in two; bottles would pop beneath the heavy tractor tyres. All the while the driver roared on, unfazed by the dangerous mess he travelled over. There was something in all this, in coming close to this huge stinking tangle. Like that view of the broken TV, it was a glimpse of the workings, the sanctioned mess that allowed for everything else to carry on smoothly and uncluttered. Into it, we might throw our old things, watching joyfully, sometimes sadly, as that front-end loader rumbled on over them.

And now, I have come here. Visiting this dump has always felt like progress, like action. It's hearty work to load up a hired trailer and then turf it all out, and the feeling of honest toil is aided by the nature of the rubbish. The dump isn't for the grimy stuff that goes into the bag on the roadside, not the meat trays and cotton buds and insides of the vacuum cleaner, but the result of gardening and renovations and clear-outs like

Craig's. Recently I renovated my own home, taking down a softboard ceiling, the pieces pulling away like biscuit. I ripped down wallpaper, pulled up hideous carpet and, in the garden, took a sledgehammer to two wishing wells and a birdbath, discovering that all three had been made by encasing parts of a washing machine in concrete. I took trip after trip to the dump to heave it all away, hefting that rolled-up carpet like a body, leaving these poor choices of the past behind. One day, weeding the garden, I found an old softball that was chewed and mouldering. At the dump, I drew my arm back to throw it as far and as hard as I could. It dropped somewhere into the middle of the heap with a faint swish, and at once flies rose, hovering in the air for a few seconds before landing again.

Transfer Station is the official name for this place, but hardly anyone has ever called it that. Mostly, it's the dump, sometimes the tip. Names that describe our needs only, and reveal our indifference in what happens once we've driven away. Names that don't allow for the fact that all that metal goes to scrap dealers in Wellington, ultimately to be melted down and remade as, say, shopping trolleys or girders. The glass and cardboard get recycled too of course, and the green waste churned into compost. Off to one side, in its own little area, is a collection of rubble, bricks and smashed concrete, and it also has a second life – crushed, and used in construction as a substrate to foundations, a filler on which buildings will rise. Even that general rubbish is only there temporarily. Once a day, a man drives into it with a bucket loader, scraping and scooping. Each bucket load is driven to the top of a concrete ramp, where, after being lifted high in the air, the way a wrestler readies to throw his foe, it's dropped into the back of a truck and driven to a place called Bonny Glen. A jolly name for what is in fact a mega dump, receiving the rubbish of much of the lower North Island: 130,000 tonnes a year. It will remain open for another fifty years, after which it will finally be considered full. Its contents then left to rot, or not as the case may be. Plastic, noted a report by the Ministry for the Environment, is the great archaeological marker of our age. Imagine some future archaeologist painstakingly brushing away soil to reveal a one-thousand-year-old disposable nappy, a discovery they then repeat, repeat and repeat for the rest of their career. But this is an optimistic vision, maybe, with its certainty that our society will exist and be able to support fields like archaeology one thousand years from now, and its assumption that if it does, people will view our era as worthy of study, worthy of anything other than contempt.

Another report by the Ministry for the Environment has estimated that if you average it out, New Zealanders each take 54 kilograms of rubbish to the dump a year. A further 153 kilos is taken, per person, from the kerbside. But these estimates were made in 2009. The amount we throw out has grown since; our mountain of rubbish rises ever higher, and all of it, like everything we do, producing greenhouse gases.

We drive away from the dump, leaving those unwanted things behind, but perhaps one day the drive will be shorter, the edge of the dump creeping closer. Within a single week, I read about a fire raging for days in the country's largest landfill, the foul smoke affecting people 10 kilometres away, and about the washing away of a West Coast dump by floodwaters, carrying decades worth of rubbish down rivers and out to the seashore. We know there are rubbish gyres swirling in the Pacific, Atlantic and Indian Oceans, vortexes in which the water is clouded with minute particles of old plastic. Some scientists believe that by 2050 the oceans will contain more plastic than fish. And so we remember, when we can, to take our own bags to the supermarket. I have stopped buying cling-film.

*

Sometimes, Thomas said, he'll see people socialising at the tip face. Sitting in his kiosk, he'll look out and there they are talking away for a good half hour. One man, he told me, came with his daughter to look at the dump's resident cats. The guy didn't pay anything, didn't dump anything, just toured so they could take a look at them all. Leaving the dump, Thomas's regulars tooted the horn, and everyone rolled up onto the slightly wobbly concrete pad where they were weighed a second time and charged for the difference. Ten dollars the minimum fee for which unwanted things will leave your life forever. They were happy to hand it over and get a joke from Thomas in exchange. 'Hot enough for you,' he said to one customer. 'Turn your heater down,' he said to another, a man in a black ute.

'Huh?'

'Turn your heater down,' he said again.

This time the man got the joke and they both laughed at it, at the idea that his little dashboard heater might be running on a day like that, pumping out enough heat to warm the whole world.

# The Adventures of Bernard Shapiro

When the Christchurch *Press* came across him in 2005, on a roadside in Culverden, Bernard Shapiro was wearing canvas trousers, an oilskin jacket, puttees and a pith helmet. He carried, among other things, a bayonet, a pipe and biltong, and was walking to Greymouth, taking the ancient freightways used by South Island Māori in their search for pounamu. The *Press* snapped a few photos, one of which they'd use again four years later, when Shapiro was charged with unlawfully possessing weapons and explosives. But in 2005 the journey was the story. 'On Wednesday night he slept under canvas by the Balmoral Forest,' the article began. '[He] began yesterday's hike with a slap-up breakfast at the Hurunui Hotel – and a beer.' This walk was the first of several expeditions that Shapiro would mount, sometimes alone, sometimes with a support crew barrelling ahead to set up camp and cook him dinner, but always in the attire of the past, evoking a general old-timeyness rather than a specific year. For one expedition his gear might be pre-World War Two, for another it would be restricted to the years immediately after, but it never went beyond the days of dun-coloured clothing, pith helmets and pipes. For that first trip to Greymouth, it was the gold rush that he sought to emulate. 'I read about these chaps who, along with a Māori guide, bimbled through – would have nearly died of starvation if it wasn't for their guide – but made it back and I thought, oh I wouldn't mind having a go at that myself.' And so he did, dressing and outfitting himself for that era, an experiment in learning details that never make to the pages of the history books: the heft and chafe of a leather pack strapped to your back, the feeling of wind and sun through layers of canvas and wool. At one point he came to a swollen river, the water churned café au lait. The New Zealand Death was the name given to drowning in the days Shapiro was wanting to re-live, a reference to the many, many settlers who lost their lives trying to cross swift rivers. But still he staggered on in his antique outfit. He felt the rush of the water and his heart beating hard, and it was then that he knew he'd found what he was looking for: an old-fashioned adventure.

I first learnt of Shapiro after a trip he took the very next year, walking through backblocks Otago. Again, he was snapped by the *Press* – he was his own best publicist. It noted that he'd be joined by members of the Ōamaru Historical Society. 'Almost all of their clothing and equipment dates from before 1957,' the story said. I read this and wondered at that 'before 1957'. It all seemed both specific and vague. There was no indication that he was recreating any particular event, and it's doubtful anyone would have walked that way at that point in time, what with highways and cars in existence by then. 'What's the point,' a friend said when I told him about it, and at once I agreed. There really was no point.

But it lingered with me, too, perhaps because I had once

daydreamed about escapes into the past myself, during teenage years spent writhing with doubt and confusion. It was the mid-1990s, those days of grunge, raves, and jeans that might double as a family tent, and to me there seemed no way in, nothing of this that I might grab and make my own. I found the music abrasive. I didn't see any coherence in the clothes. A classmate turned up for mufti day in dungarees, and I watched, waiting for everyone to laugh. Instead they asked where he bought them. Dungarees! I couldn't figure this out at all, and it was then that I began to look elsewhere, finding solace in old things, in books and movies from decades gone by. I was a film buff, I told myself, but really it was the past I was watching – the clothes and music and interiors of times that were trapped in celluloid and able to be studied from the safety of my bedroom. When I finished *Vertigo*, Alfred Hitchcock's great study of obsession, I immediately hit rewind and watched it all over again. Not so that I might relive its twists or the strange relationship at its core, but merely to see Jimmy Stewart once more driving through 1950s San Francisco in his DeSoto sedan. His dark suit, the streets of drug stores, newsagents and department stores – it was more vivid, more appealing than 1990s Christchurch. I began to mooch in op shops looking for artefacts. I bought a pinstripe suit that had the wide trousers and rigid shoulders of the 1940s, and wore it to a friend's party, imagining that I could somehow exist in that world and this at the same time.

By the time I read of Shapiro's story, I had long given up on this impossible hope and come to an uneasy peace with the present, but it made some sense to me still. I would recognise the common theme in articles that cropped up about him over the years: a desert expedition, tales of historic camping in Arthur's Pass. Driving to my mother's house in Christchurch one day, I watched a man hoon by in a World War Two jeep and disappear down a driveway. I craned my neck as I passed, and could just see the man, in khaki shorts, jumping out with a grin big enough to see from afar. It must be that guy, I realised as I drove on.

One other thing Shapiro wore on those expeditions, and still wore when I met him at his house in Banks Peninsula, was a moustache. It was wide and sandy, the sort of Edwardian facial hair that, properly oiled and tended, became de rigueur for baristas for a while there, but which Shapiro wore slightly limp at the edges, authentically tattered. It was camouflage, he reckoned. His teeth were in bad shape, because for years he couldn't afford a dentist. 'It has been a pauper's life for me, but it's been an honest one,' he told me, and similarly quaint phrasing cropped up often in our conversation. There was much mention of 'chaps' and 'lasses', and at times I was reminded of the preambles given by the clients in Sherlock Holmes's consulting room, life stories framed within Victorian values. 'I've always been poor apart from now, but this isn't my wealth. This is Amy's wealth,' he said, referring to his wife, and their home, the raised deck on which he and I sat, the dog panting beside us in the peninsula's dry heat. Inside was the usual family clutter – kids' toys, plates and papers – as well as the less usual: a shelf of pipes, pictures of the Queen.

For decades now, Shapiro has made his living playing the French horn. The day before we spoke, he had been rehearsing *Tosca* with the Christchurch Symphony Orchestra. His musical instincts were brilliant, conductor Marc Taddei would tell me. Music was a love that had once been a crutch, a retreat from the bullies of his childhood. He was a weedy kid who cried too easily, Shapiro said, and he told me about this, and about his adoptive parents – two Jewish New Yorkers who came to New Zealand via Fiji – and his wife, kids and biological mum, who was a minor star of New Zealand television in the 1970s. Interesting stuff sure, but throughout I found myself waiting for the link, the explanation of where the past fit into all of this. It was the reason I had sought him out, had driven across the parched countryside to find him. Where had this habit of traipsing into the wilderness in colonial garb come from? When I asked straight out, Shapiro was matter-of-fact. It was purely about recreating history he said, and insisted I stand in his study and examine his library of high adventure, New Zealand and military history in order to see the inspiration for it all, as if his walks were a natural extension of his reading. He was wearing a pith helmet that day, he said, only because it was a damn good sunhat. And yet he changed hats twice that afternoon, greeting me by his driveway in a straw boater and, at one point, doffing a battered lemon squeezer. When I suggested a photo, he took a pose immediately, sitting on the bonnet of his jeep with his pipe in hand.

Feeling the need for a second opinion, I rang one of the men who had accompanied Shapiro on that Otago walk, Michael O'Brien, a bookbinder and brewer from Ōamaru, and, as if making a dirty phone call, asked him what he was wearing. Tweed, he said. A three-button suit, boots and a linen shirt. A gold watch sat snug in his waistcoat pocket. 'I can be longwinded,' he warned me, and like Shapiro, he spoke at length and with little prompting about his life and his interests. The two had met through an organisation called Alf's Imperial Army. Founded by the Christchurch Wizard in the early 70s, Alf's is in decline now, but in its heyday, members dressed as British Redcoats circa 1880 to hold mock battles with paper swords and flour bombs. Shapiro was a poor fit for Alf's, O'Brien said. Despite the anarchic, Monty Pythonesque tone of its website ('ALF's Imperial Army stands for all that is British and is silly'), O'Brien described a fairly rigid organisation, and Shapiro 'just wouldn't wear red and behave himself and take orders'. A similar clash occurred on the Otago trip: that 'pre-1957' noted by the *Press* had been Shapiro's deadline only. The others were dressed, at O'Brien's instigation, as Jacobite Scots, the clansmen who fought to restore Bonnie Prince Charlie to the English throne and who died in large numbers in 1746 on the field of Culloden. O'Brien called his group 'Chieftains of the Pudding Race', after a line from Burns, and was unhappy to see Shapiro turn up dressed, as he put it, like 'Crocodile Dundee'.

For all that, he had much in common with Shapiro. Both spoke against the thin pleasures and short attention spans of the modern world, and of their own lousy younger years. Both were adopted, and it's tempting to read much into this, as if this common origin were the key to their interests, both combing the past for connection to missing family. But then again, all kinds of people dwell on the past. Me, for example, or perhaps some of the other members of O'Brien's group: Big Ken, Wee Jock the piper ('extremely unreliable,' said O'Brien), or the man from Invercargill, nicknamed Slim, who had converted to Islam. In their kilts, they walked on with Bernard, losing people as they went to blistered feet, unreliability (Jock, naturally), and the need to go back to work, until there were only four who made it to Danseys Pass, and it was Bernard alone, the man in khaki, who made it all the way to Arrowtown.

As I had hoped, once he got around to the subject, O'Brien was more forthcoming about his motivations. Protest was one reason he gave for his outfit. His Scots garb was a statement against what he saw as lack of commitment among many locals to the goal of Ōamaru's Victorian heritage quarter. People wore modern glasses with period clothes, skirts made of old tablecloths. It was just dress-ups for them. Property developers lurked behind the whole thing, he said, looking at how they might make a quick buck. 'I'd get up in the morning and when I got dressed, I felt like I was putting my battle clothing on to go out in the world.' This theme of revolt and rebellion came up often. As a teenager in the 70s, he had been an outsider in stodgy old provincial New Zealand. 'An unlikely person,' he said. 'I was pretty afraid of girls, a nerdish boy who stayed at home and painted soldiers and collected British medals and listened to BBC World Service and the Russian one, and the Chinese one, stuff like that, on a valve radio in my room.' Hope came with punk and then post-punk – subcultures that pulled the fingers at everything he'd hated about that decade: its daggy palette of brown and burnt orange, its reliance on American culture. But when fashions changed, and those same punks put on the checked shirts of the grunge era, he felt it as a personal betrayal. He began his own rebellion by looking backwards, moving through the 1950s and the 1930s, then settling, but for that stint in 1740s Scotland, in the Victorian/ Edwardian era. He took inspiration from William Morris, the Victorian advocate for craftsmanship, and in this, and many things, he was a stickler. He got wound up talking about people in baseball caps. He brought a friend's child to tears by hiding their puffer jacket. He acted as a sort of out-of-fashion police, with jurisdiction over the greater Ōamaru area.

It was later, long after talking to Shapiro and O'Brien, that I would find another exploration of this backward-looking impulse. It was a book by American writer Jenny Thompson about war reenactors, a pastime Shapiro had dabbled with. Thompson had spent seven years with these men – they were almost exclusively men – watching as they spent their weekends recreating the Battle of the Bulge and, more often than not, squabbling over the authenticity of their uniforms. Many spoke of it the way Shapiro had, as an exercise in reliving the past. But Thompson viewed this explanation as a dodge. 'It is a contemporary practice,' she insisted. On the surface those reenactors may have appeared to be opting out of the present, some even going as far making their own, period-accurate magazines and packaging, but opting out was impossible. They were still inhabitants of today, she argued. Their interest could only be a product of or maybe a response to the world they lived in now. Then but now, in this modern version of the past, they might find what was otherwise missing from their lives. Camaraderie and adventure, were two examples Thompson gave. Shapiro had found both, from what he told me, and to those I'd add an overlapping third: identity. I was thinking here of my own out-of-step adolescence, of those days when I had looked backwards for clues to who I might be. It seemed to me that both men had done something similar, albeit more decisively and more successfully than I had. Rather than try and fail to make their way as part of the present as I do now, fumbling with pop culture, still half-glancing to the past, they had taken archetypes from a dusty shelf: O'Brien a craftsman of the old school, turning his bookpress in a white stone building; Bernard the explorer, the adventurer, roaring into the wilderness with a pith helmet on his head.

'What a year it's been in classical music!' wrote Melinda Bargreen of the *Seattle Times*. In December 2007, she had put together a listicle proving that classical musicians 'can behave just as badly, and as oddly, as anyone else'. There was a brawl at the Boston Pops, and an oboist in Washington DC had been caught running a betting ring. New Zealanders cropped up twice in this dishonour roll, fulfilling the usual boast that we punch above our weight. Kiri Te Kanawa had been sued for backing out of her appearance in a John Farnham show. The reason for her change of heart? She'd watched one of his performances. 'I was concerned about the knickers or underpants and underwear apparel being thrown at him and him collecting it and obviously holding it in his hands as some sort of trophy,' she told a court. And then there was Shapiro, second on Bargreen's list. 'French horn bearing arms,' she wrote, before noting that he'd been charged with 'possessing a cache of "military-style" explosives'.

Technically, he'd been charged with possessing weapons he wasn't licensed for, but on that list of charges were some eye-catching words: mine, grenade launcher. He had explosives stored on top of his fridge. The story was picked up by the *Press* and the *Herald*, before eventually coming to the attention of the *Seattle Times*. It was referred to on a TV panel show, and talkback hosts John Tamihere and Willie Jackson had a lot of fun diagnosing Shapiro as a psychopath, a sociopath and a 'Hannibal Lecter'.

In Shapiro's version, it was a case of naivety, of trust misplaced, and once again he evoked a quaint, old notion: the code of honour. He told me he had met a man who'd recently surrendered his firearms licence but didn't want to give up his weapons. Because Shapiro had a licence, the man asked if he'd look after them for him. 'I'd known him for years, so I said sure.' He took on the weapons, and later, shortly before he was due to leave for Australia on a chamber concert tour, the man asked him to look after some ammunition as well. 'He turned up and I really didn't have time to sort it through or say no or anything like that. I was weak. I just said sure, put it there and I'll secure it. I did not look into another man's private gear.'

The police got wind of this, and he found himself in court. The case dragged on, extended at one point when his lawyer injured himself skiing. Many hours were spent debating those weapons. The grenade launcher turned out to be a flare gun, the mines were of a kind used for training. The charges he faced were, according to the judge, 'a raft of technical stratagems', and although found guilty of some, he was ultimately discharged without conviction. Still, the publicity would do serious damage to his career, and prompted people on the street to call him a monster. It was also, it seemed to me, a case of that persona of his coming to clash with the modern world. The free-wheeling, gun-toting adventurer of old was a bad fit for modern gun-licence regulations, just as O'Brien had found bookbinding to be a less than lucrative trade over the years.

The experience had left Shapiro reclusive, he said, implying he was reduced, no longer his old self. And yet, in the years following, he planned more expeditions, bigger than any before, beginning with an attempt to retrace the route of the Long Range Desert Group, a British reconnaissance unit from World War Two that had included many New Zealanders. Shapiro gathered his own desert group together, and they rehearsed, wearing itchy serge uniforms and driving long distances in vintage military vehicles, including his own 1943 Jeep. 'Everything was there,' he told me. They had the gear, they had men with nicknames like Chalkie and Algie, and they had a route planned that covered Egypt, Libya and Algeria. It took in the White Desert, the Black Desert and the Great Sand Sea, the oasis at Siwa and the Qattara

Depression. It was to be a great and grand adventure. But it never happened. While they were planning to recreate history, others got busy making it. The Arab Spring erupted, and their destination became a battlefield again. 'No one would insure us,' Shapiro said. 'If we'd gone through there we probably would have had to put something large and noisy on the back of the jeep.'

For his next attempt at adventure, he teamed up with a friend, Andrew Hewson; the twist this time was that it would be an expedition they shared. They made a documentary about Shapiro and two others trekking through the Mackenzie Country, a 200-kilometre walk from Mount Cook to Kurow. Naturally they wore tweed and wool, and carried World War Two-era packs. In bad weather they donned canvas rain capes, and for sustenance they chewed biltong. 'Biltong is excellent because it provides you with the salt and potassium that your body is getting rid of when you're sweating like mad.' There was whisky for the end of the day, provided as sponsorship by Ōamaru's Single Malt Company; an image of Shapiro remains on their website.

While they walked, a support crew in World War Two-era vehicles, Shapiro's jeep among them, travelled on ahead to set up canvas tents, fold-out chairs and stretcher beds, bring water, hunt rabbits, and even whitewash rocks with which they could demarcate the campsite. Their chef organised a field kitchen, cooked dinner and baked bannock, a dense, flat bread. In this way, Shapiro and company crossed the Dalgety Range and the Mackenzie Basin. 'There is no tussock in the middle of it, it is just dust, bones, and that's all that's out there.' They encountered snow at Mount Cook homestead, and ran into a storm, and throughout it all they gathered footage for their documentary, which they would pitch to TVNZ. 'It wasn't reality TV, it was real TV,' Shapiro said. 'It was done with a passion and there was poetry and there was beauty and there was art and there was the most incredible scenery, shot brilliantly by this young chap Andrew Hewson . . . And they didn't want it.'

Not long after, TVNZ came out with an historic adventure series of their own, *First Crossings*. For this, hosts Kevin Biggar and Jamie Fitzgerald reenacted actual journeys from New Zealand history. Both men were veterans of a transatlantic rowing race, and they had once trekked to the South Pole, but Shapiro remained sniffy. 'They stayed in hotels,' he said, 'whereas we were sleeping on the ground with wool blankets. They didn't walk to their sites, they flew there by helicopter and pretended they had been hard men.' This was the angriest he got in our hours of conversation. Nothing else, not even his courtroom battle, would elicit as much emotion as the spectacle of two men reenacting the past in a way that was, in his eyes, inauthentic.

With the windscreen folded down, Shapiro's jeep rushed down gravel, skidding to a stop so I could jump out and get my blown-away hat, before taking off again. There was a distinctive growl to the engine which, if you're over a certain age, sounds like one thing: *M\*A\*S\*H*. I thought of Alan Alda, of meatball surgery and that mournful clarinet theme as we hurtled on. My nostalgia suddenly broke when Shapiro twisted the wheel and we flew off the road and into bush, smashing and crashing through scrub. 'You should have seen your face,' he said, laughing when we came to a stop. It was a comment I resented – with the windscreen down I could have been pierced by a stray branch. And for that moment, I felt my patience with him and this persona of his dissipate; I saw it all as performance. In my irritation I echoed a comment I had seen on a story Shapiro once wrote for *Stuff* about camping in Arthur's Pass. The story was full of his usual references to canvas and whisky and jeeps, and beneath it someone had accused Shapiro of living in a world of his own. Shapiro himself had responded to this. 'Better my world than yours,' he wrote. 'I have nice things to say about people.' This was true. But for that bitterness over *First Crossings*, he was unfailingly positive, wistful at most about the failure of his North Africa trip, his lengthy and expensive court case and the damage it had done to his career. I had begun to trace this litany of things gone wrong, only to think them all small when Shapiro told me of his latest setback. He had been diagnosed with Ménière's disease, a disorder of the inner ear which would eventually cause hearing loss. It is incurable. He had told me this before we hopped in the jeep, again smiling as he told the story, shrugging off the end of what had been most of a lifetime as an accomplished musician.

Of course, he was planning another trip. He asked that I not share the details. 'Despite that setback,' I might have written – except that I had come to believe it was a case of 'because', not 'despite'. Surely the need to light out with an ancient pack on his pack was helping him to get past those blows. No matter what happened, he would always be who he wanted to be by simply donning his hat and setting off into the countryside with a pipe in his mouth. 'There's not that many people who live out their dreams and aspirations this much,' his friend, the filmmaker Andrew Hewson, had told me. In his mind, Shapiro's persona was less a case of mimicry than something closer to discovery. 'It's like he's uncovered actually who he is on an honest, healthy level.' I liked this idea and, but for that moment in the jeep, I had liked Shapiro. At one point I had warned him that nothing might come of our conversation. I couldn't say for sure that I'd be able to write anything but had simply come to see him with notebook in hand, chasing something that had struck me as curious. 'It doesn't matter,' he said, and I realised immediately that if anyone understood, he would. And so we talked on and on, him generous with his time, generous generally. In his jeep, he found a leather canister, a map holder that he had forgotten he owned. 'Do you want this?' he said, and when he spotted a double of one of his books, he offered that to me too: John A. Lee's *Shiner Slattery*, yarns about a swagman who once tramped New Zealand's backroads. I declined the map holder but took the book. I left him holding his calabash pipe beside his jeep at the end of a long gravel road, plotting away, thinking of the next trip. It wasn't till much later that I would open Lee's book and find on the very first page: 'Romance never exists in the moment of life, but lies to the rear, in the days when we did, or ahead in the days when we shall.' Bernard, it seemed to me, had found a way to combine both.

One day, a long time ago, I spent an afternoon the way I spent many then, browsing in a junk shop. I came across an old book, the cover a photograph of a city skyline in the same sun-soaked Technicolor tones as those streets in *Vertigo*. It was a manual for writers, this book, a compendium of contact details for Manhattan literary agents, and submission specs for magazines with names like *Stag* and *Men's Weekly* which accepted short stories in the 'Hemingway mode'. Clearly this book was out of date, useless. But still it made its way into my daydreams, and I told myself that the words in it had meaning, that maybe they represented some corner of the past that might be lived now. One evening I sat at a desk in my bedroom with a record playing on my mother's stereo, music that I thought best fit the Hemingway mode: Herb Alpert's *The Lonely Bull*. The slow, solemn parp of Mexican-themed easy listening. It evoked the fatal drama of the bullring, the lonely life of a writer. And as it played, I sat at my desk and wrote. I was, I imagined, a writer.

# These Ghosts

Ghosts hang around old cemeteries, old houses, our one castle. They haunt the ruins of lunatic asylums. They are suicides and jilted lovers. They are the victims of murder. They are common in old theatres it seems: Auckland's Civic, Wellington's St James and its Opera House, Christchurch Court Theatre – all have their ghosts. These are the usual places. London's Drury Lane is crowded with ghosts. Old buildings need to be haunted. Once enough time has passed, they come with a figure in Victorian dress at the end of a hallway, something tap-tapping on the walls. A ghost is patina, it is a marker from Historic Places. The oldest buildings still standing here, Mission House and the Stone Store, are among our most haunted.

But there is another kind of haunting, one that feels particular to these islands. The kind that feeds on the loneliness of our spaces. These ghosts haunt forestry towns and windswept coasts, farm houses and whare out back of beyond. They are in the bush and empty clearings. The presence of Cedric, the ghost of a hunter lost in the Tararua Ranges, can be felt within the tramping hut he never returned to in life. These ghosts are drowned men walking the length of a West Coast beach. They are a dog that wanders sand dunes after someone has died, a fire on a beach at night, an ageing interisland ferry possessed of the need to turn back for Wellington while struggling against stormy seas.

I have been reading about these, possessed myself by a whim. Recently I went to my local library and took out the few books they held about New Zealand ghosts. It was a slim selection. Mine was an incomplete survey, and in this it mirrored a childhood attempt to create a compendium of ghost stories. I was a nerd for the supernatural then and so were my friends. I borrowed the books they had on the subject of real-life ghosts and tried to copy them out in an exercise book – my own ghostipedia, except I got only as far as painstakingly transcribing an article about actor Telly Savalas's claim that he'd once hitched a ride with a stranger who spoke in an eerie falsetto – the ghost of a man who'd shot himself in the throat. 'I'll give you a ride,' he'd shrieked, and Kojak hopped in.

This time I had no grand ambitions, and nor was I believer. I read simply for the chill of a good ghost story, and had little interest in attempts at giving shadows and muffled sounds the hard edges of fact. This distinction made much of this reading hard going. The writers of the ghost books I found tried to corroborate these stories, they offered evidence. To read Julie Miller and Grant Osborn's *Unexplained New Zealand* was to learn that a speck of dust on a camera lens was in fact an ectoplasmic orb, and that grainy black-and-white images of reflection or shadow were all open to the wildest possible interpretation: a demented skull face in a shower stall, a woman's head on the body of an insect, a ghost coming through the wall. I have looked at these pictures till cross-eyed without seeing these things, but there was a time when I would have seen it all. Behind that boyhood attempt at a ghost compendium was the desire to be a ghost hunter, a seeker of such proof. Once, back then, I discovered a book on this subject in the library and shared key passages with my nan when staying over one night. It was British, this book, a large hardback by some fusty chap with a beard, and, like Miller and Osborn, he included advice on ghost-hunting methods.

'If someone says they've seen a ghost, you need to make sure they're not drunk,' I told Nan from my grandfather's bed, the twin to hers – he had been demoted to the spare room.

'Is that right dear,' she said from beneath a candlewick counterpane.

I remember too that this book held a chapter on tools of the trade, the necessary equipment of the ghost hunter, but only one item stuck with me, the suggestion of a carpet bag for lugging the gear and, as a result, for the longest time, the words 'carpet bag' carried an aura, they hinted at the dark mysteries of the occult.

To read this type of thing again now was to discover that the ghosts are the anti-climax. They punctuate, they create the ending – but the story is in the setting. Those empty beaches, those whare. In Grant Shanks and Tahu Potiki's *Where No Birds Sing*, the titular story has no ghost at all, just a remote valley in the Fiordland bush that holds a sense of dread, is so unsettling that a deer would rather take its chances with a hunter's gun than enter. They appeared to working people, these ghosts, to rural people. A skim of Shanks and Potiki's book finds reference to the freezing works and a fruit-processing plant, a timber mill and an army base. Worlds of beer by the jug, of bring a plate and borrow the trailer. These were the ghosts of old-fashioned, provincial New Zealand, a place that often gets viewed, if at all, through the rear-view mirror.

We like to think of ourselves as an urban people now, with flash jobs, sophisticated tastes. The beach, the bach, the bush have become clichés, sanitised, the subjects of advertising campaigns. Imagining them as haunted spaces offers us a way to see them again. It reminds us of the old tradition of New Zealand Gothic, our infamous unease. What is a ghost but loneliness amplified? A ghost never appears before a crowd. Ghosts are uncertainty too, the sense of something gone before, something bad, reminders of those New Zealand deaths: drowning, suicide, violence, or staggering lost and hopeless as the bush grows cold.

Shanks and Potiki begin their anthology with a description of Māori spirituality, of the concepts of mana and tapu, and pre-colonial burial practices. 'I offer this background as introduction to the stories that follow, not as an explanation for them,' Potiki writes, but many of the apparitions and happenings that follow are explained, often vaguely, in terms of a pre-European past. A family is cursed after building a house near a burial site, another spots a fire on a beach at night but in the morning there is nothing to show for it. The spot, it is suggested, was once a gathering place for Māori war parties. In a piece for the *Paris Review*, Jennifer Wilson writes of American ghost stories as counters to 'national historic amnesia', and refers to tales of haunted slave plantations and that hoary old trope of the Indian burial ground. About the latter, she quotes author Colin Dickey: 'The narrative of the haunted Indian burial ground hides a certain anxiety about the land on which Americans – specifically white, middle-class Americans – live.'

And so it is here, too: these ghosts are Pākehā angst that this land has a longer history, had earlier owners and occupants, meanings now unknown. The vagueness with which the stories are explained is appropriate, then; the usual national state of blithe ignorance about this past, revealed in twilight moments, is cover for our fear.

I see now that for me, reading ghost stories has also been an exercise in nostalgia, an attempt to revisit a time when ghost hunting seemed a viable career option and Nan was still around to encourage me. The world promised mystery and I had yet to learn that what you see is what you get: home to work to home again, putting the rubbish bags out, waiting for the jug to boil. Closing the book, the ghosts disappear. Stepping out of the library, back out into small town streets, I leave them behind.

And yet, when I hear the floorboards creak at night, I know it's just what floorboards in old houses do, but still I find myself thinking about the old man who lived here before me, struggling alone as the grass grew high and his mind went soft until finally they took him away and he died soon after. From the windows you can see, as he must have, the mountains where I sometimes go tramping, and where, stepping into the bush at night, everything a shade of black, looming, empty and lonely, I hurry back to the hut and my tramping companions. I don't believe in ghosts. I do believe, though, in this land of ghosts.

# Select Bibliography

Bargreen, Melinda. 'Classical world had plenty of weirdness in 2007'. *The Seattle Times*, 23 Dec. 2007.

Belich, James. *Paradise Reforged: A History of the New Zealanders from the 1880s to the Year 2000*. Auckland: Allen Lane / Penguin Press, 2001.

Calder, Mick and Janet Tyson. *Meat Acts: The New Zealand Meat Industry 1972–1997*. Wellington: Meat New Zealand, 1999.

Campbell, Russell. *Sedition – The Suppression of Dissent in World War II New Zealand* [film]. Vanguard Films, 2005.

Crean, Mike. 'Shapiro takes a walk to revisit the past'. *Christchurch Press*, 27 Dec. 2005.

Dickey, Colin. *Ghostland: An American History in Haunted Places*. New York: Penguin Books, 2017.

Dunmore, John. *Norman Kirk: A Portrait*. Palmerston North: New Zealand Books, 1972.

Dyne, Dudley G. *Famous N.Z. Murders*. Auckland: Fontana Silver Fern, 1974.

Frame, Janet. *Owls Do Cry*. Melbourne: Sun Books, 1976.

Grant, David. *The Mighty Totara: The Life and Times of Norman Kirk*.

Auckland: Random House, 2014.

—*Out in the Cold: Pacifists and Conscientious Objectors in New Zealand during World War II*. Auckland: Reed Methuen, 1986.

Greene, Graham. *A Sort of Life*. London: Bodley Head, 1971.

Gundry, Sheridan. *Making a Killing: A History of the Gisborne-East Coast Freezing Works Industry*. Gisborne: Tairawhiti Museum, 2004.

Gustafson, Barry. *Kiwi Keith: A Biography of Keith Holyoake*. Auckland: Auckland University Press, 2007.

Hayward, Dai (ed). *Golden Jubilee: The Story of the First Fifty Years of the New Zealand Meat Producers Board 1922-1972*. Wellington: Universal Printers Ltd, 1972.

Hayward, Margaret. *Diary of the Kirk Years*. Queen Charlotte Sound and Wellington: Cape Catley Limited and Reed, 1981.

Joyce, James. *A Portrait of the Artist as a Young Man*. Introduction and notes by J.S. Atherton. London: Heinemann Educational Books, 1967.

Lee, John A. *Shiner Slattery*. Auckland: Collins, 1964.

McGibbon, Ian. *New Zealand's Vietnam War: A History of Combat, Commitment and Controversy*. Auckland: Exisle, 2010.

Miller, Julie and Grant Osborn. *Unexplained New Zealand: Ghosts, UFOs and Mysterious Creatures*. Auckland: Reed, 2007.

Morrieson, Ronald Hugh. *Pallet on the Floor*. Auckland: Penguin, 1983.

Neale, Tom. *An Island to Oneself*. London – Sydney: Collins, 1966.

Nelson, Bill. 'Wild Talking: The Art of the Tramping Conversation'. *Up Country*, upcountry.co.nz/wild_talking.html. Accessed 31 May 2019.

Orwell, George. *Shooting an Elephant and Other Essays*. London: Penguin, 2003.

Page, Stuart. 'The truth about the Skeptics' A.F.F.C.O. Video'. *SPLEEN*, vital.org.nz/stu.html. Accessed 31 May 2019.

Pearson, Bill. *Fretful Sleepers and Other Essays*. Auckland: Heinemann Educational Books, 1974.

Pratt, John. *The Prison Diary of A.C. Barrington: Dissent and Conformity in Wartime New Zealand*. Dunedin: Otago University Press, 2016.

Rabel, Roberto. *New Zealand and the Vietnam War*. Auckland: Auckland University Press, 2005.

Schweid, Richard. *Eel*. London: Reaktion Books, 2009.

Shanks, Grant and Tahu Potiki. *Where No Birds Sing: Tales of the Supernatural in Aotearoa*. Christchurch: Shoal Bay Press, 1998.

Skeptics. 'AFFCO'. YouTube, uploaded by Flying Nun Records, 11 February 2014, www.youtube.com/watch?v=qZKDjElk7Ts. Accessed 25 March 2021.

Summers, John. *Dreamscape 1*. Christchurch: Pisces Print, 1991.

—*Dreamscape 2*. Christchurch: Pisces Print, 1993.

—*Strictly for the Words*. Christchurch: Pisces Print, 1974.

Taylor, Rowan and Ian Smith. *The State of New Zealand's Environment 1997*. Wellington: Ministry for the Environment and GP Publications, 1997.

Thompson, Jenny. *War Games: Inside the World of Twentieth-Century War Reenactors*. Washington: Smithsonian Books, 2004.

Waste Not Consulting. *Household Sector Waste to Landfall in New Zealand.* Prepared for Ministry for Environment, 2009, mfe.govt. nz/publications/waste/household-sector-waste-landfill-new-zealand. Accessed 25 March 2021.

White, Pat. *Planting the Olives & Other Essential Acts.* Frontiers Press, 2004.

Whybrew, Christine. *'Art is an Act of Life': The Making of the John and Connie Summers Collection of New Zealand Art.* 2001, University of Canterbury, MA Thesis.

Wilson, Jennifer. 'In Russia, the Ultimate Scary Story is about Losing Your Coat'. *Paris Review,* 31 October 2019, theparisreview.org/ blog/2019/10/31/in-russia-the-ultimate-scary-story-is-about-losing-your-coat/. Accessed 25 March 2021.

Wolfe, Richard. *A Short History of Sheep in New Zealand.* Auckland: Random House, 2006.

# Acknowledgements

I am very grateful to everyone who shared their stories with me and particular mention is owed to Stella Neale, Uncle Dale, Philip Dobb, my aunts Faith and Bronwen, Linda Haddon, Michael Shale, Paul Melser, Bernard Shapiro and Michael O'Brien. I would also like to recognise the Bell family for their encouraging words. My uncle Llew passed away since I spoke to him for 'Temperament' and I remain grateful for the time that researching this piece gave me in his always interesting company.

For several years I have belonged to a writing group consisting of very talented people whose advice and comments have directly helped with many of these pieces and, indirectly, everything I write.

Thank you to Creative NZ for a grant to work on this. I was also recipient of a D'Arcy Writers Grant, which gave me the time and confidence to write 'Temperament'. I am thankful to both the judging panel and to Mark and Deborah D'Arcy.

Several of these pieces appeared the following publications: *North & South*, *The Spinoff*, *Newsroom*, *Sport*, *Sunday Star-Times* and *Turbine*. I am thankful to the editors of all but will single out Steve Braunias for his consistent encouragement and for awarding me a two-night stay at Auckland's Surrey Hotel (roast meal included), during which I worked on what would become two of these essays.

Thank you to Fergus Barrowman, Kirsten McDougall and the rest of the team at Victoria University Press, particularly Ashleigh Young for making this a better book.

Thank you to my parents, my friends (the tramping buddies of 'Amateurs') and again, to Alisa for her support and patience. This book is dedicated to her and to Henry Zhan, who both make this life complete.